ALLIED DUNBAR

RETIREMENT PLANNING GUIDE

by

Barry Bean
Bill Tadd
and
Dr H Beric Wright

© Allied Dunbar Financial Services Limited 1991

ISBN 0 85121 7346

Published by

Longman Law, Tax and Finance
Longman Group UK Limited
21–27 Lamb's Conduit Street, London WC1N 3NJ

Associated Offices

Australia, Hong Kong, Malaysia, Singapore, USA

A CIP catalogue record for this book is available from the British Library.

Printed in Great Britain by Biddles of Guildford.

About the authors

Barry Bean is a senior manager with The Bridford Group Ltd, an independent financial planning, pensions and insurance broking company. Bridford is part of Clark Whitehill, a leading firm of chartered accountants. For the past ten years Barry has specialised in personal financial planning, pensions and retirement advice. He is also a contributor to professional magazines on financial planning and related subjects.

Bill Tadd is currently Director of the Institute of Journalists and also organises Retirement Planning Courses. He is a former news editor of the *The Daily Telegraph* and Financial Editor of *Choice* magazine.

Dr H Beric Wright, MB, FRCS, MFOM, is a consultant in Health and Retirement. Now himself retired, he was the Founder of the Institute of Directors Medical Centre (which later became the BUPA Medical Centre) and a Director of BUPA until 1985. He has written and lectured extensively on health matters. Author of *Executive Ease and Dis-Ease* published in 1975 he explains the relationship between stress and illness. A second book, *Are You Managing Your Health?* published earlier this year, develops this theme.

Acknowledgement

As is usually the case, a book rarely emerges having been the sole work of one person, and this book is no exception. I would like to thank Tony Foreman for his financial help – which is always willingly given. Also, my thanks to Dr Beric Wright who provides essential balance to the subject of retirement planning in the last three chapters of the book in case we all become fixated by financial matters.

Also, welcome to Bill Tadd, who has provided additional balance to this edition with his important contribution on leisure and activities.

Finally, I am grateful to Bill Loving for his original work on accommodation in retirement which, once again, features in this new edition.

To this I must add my grateful thanks to the people at Allied Dunbar especially Vince Jerrard LLB, ACII, Stuart Reynolds LLB of the Legal Department and Clifford Green—all of whom helped this fourth edition of the book reach fruition.

Barry Bean
London
June 1991

Introduction

For most people, the basic ingredients of a happy and successful retirement are a stable environment of home, friends, interests, satisfactory health, adequate financial circumstances and a sound personal philosophy of life. Most are agreed, however, that for the majority of people approaching retirement, finance is a main concern.

There are so many things which need to be planned for: continuing an income, preserving the family home, avoiding unnecessary taxation and preventing unnecessary family disputes and turmoil. Despite the real rewards of planning for the future most problems arise, not because people have made incorrect plans but because they have made no plans at all.

A dictionary definition of retirement is not particularly encouraging. It talks of people who have retired as having 'withdrawn from society or observation'. It means to go away or retreat.

A better approach is to regard this period of perhaps up to 30 years or more as a time of independence. We can be independent of the need to turn up for work, but we have to accept that we have no automatic income and no automatic salary increases. We cannot change our independence and choose one with better prospects and perks – the independence we achieve will only be as good as the plan we have made for it.

Many people still tend to regard this part of their life as one of 'cutting back'. They tend not to see any prospect of improvement in the quality of their life. For many of us, retirement, or the thought of giving up work at all, comes as a shock.

The shock is largely due to the lack of preparation. Despite the considerable and growing publicity that has been given in recent years to the need to prepare for retirement, most people still do not.

When all is said and done, retirement should be a happy, relaxed and enjoyable time of life. Doing some sensible planning will help to achieve this objective. Your key considerations should be to:

- Draw up a budget and work out how much you will need to live on.
- Get a state pension forecast from the DSS.
- Get an occupational or private pension forecast as well. Check if you can make additional contributions if you are not providing for the maximum benefit.
- Review your investments and look at the tax position.
- Make a Will.
- Use the checklist at the back of this book to record what you own and where it is kept.
- Get advice and keep in regular contact with your adviser before and after you retire.

But there is more to retirement than just financial planning. Life is for living and retirement produces the opportunity to lead a new or different life. The challenge has to be understood, accepted and then planned for. 'How are you going to spend your time?' is as important as the 'how' of finance. This book outlines both problems.

We are all living longer. Medical care is better, we look after ourselves more with diet and exercise, modern surgery can help to refurbish some of the worn out bits – and we are retiring earlier.

It's time to start planning for it.

Contents

1 Providing for retirement

On retirement, you are likely to be able to exchange part of your pension for a sizeable cash sum, and this will need to be prudently invested. One glance at the financial pages of a Sunday newspaper will highlight the bewildering number of investment opportunities that exist, all of them promising a handsome return. Which one is best for you? This will depend on many factors, not least of which is how you stand as far as the taxman is concerned. You will need to formulate a proper investment strategy to make best use of your hard earned capital.

1.1 Some common problems

Inevitably there will be those who retire with a great deal of money and those with very little. The fortunate ones with an abundance of wealth may wish to explore how they can minimise the tax liabilities, both during their lifetime and on their death. This could mean moving abroad to a country where the tax climate is more congenial or it may simply mean arranging their affairs in such a way as to reduce the impact of UK taxation.

At the other end of the spectrum are those with too little income, and here it may be necessary to take advantage of any additional financial help that is available.

Whatever position you find yourself in, it will almost certainly be the case that proper planning will help to increase the financial security of your retirement years. This guide will help to point you in the right direction, but you may well need to seek professional advice on the best course of action for your individual circumstances. As with planning anything, the earlier you seek advice the better.

A good advisor is worth his weight in gold; he will ensure you receive the most up-to-date information on pension, tax and financial matters, and enable you to act accordingly to gain the maximum benefit.

Your financial affairs should ideally be reviewed regularly, say once a year, with the help of a professional. This will dramatically improve your chances of ending up at retirement financially well prepared for the years ahead. It will also reduce the worry that most people experience when it comes to making complicated investment decisions. A problem shared is a problem halved, especially when you have an expert on your side.

So don't let financial worries cloud your old age. Start planning early and money problems will in all probability never arise.

1.2   Drawing up a budget

The first step to sound financial planning is drawing up a budget. It is important to know where you stand. You may have had quite a lot of surplus income when you were working, now you need to budget more carefully—especially if you are retiring on a fixed income. On the other hand, don't be unnecessarily despondent: your before-tax income may go down but your after-tax income may not be so far short of the take home pay you enjoyed while working. If you manage your money carefully you may well be able to live as well—or even better—than before.

The best approach is to make a list of your expenditure by taking a year's supply of your bank statements, cheque book stubs and statements from any credit card companies (ensure as far as possible that you have identified *all* your expenditure, noting any extraordinary items that do not occur on a regular basis). When this has been done, fill in the table on page 3, making an allowance for any increase or decrease you expect to occur when you retire.

The table can be used by those who are planning some way ahead, as well as those who are about to stop working. Of course certain allowances must be made, especially by people who fall into the former category, but nevertheless it will be a useful exercise to compare your anticipated expenditure with what you expect to receive.

1.2.1 Table: Expenditure Chart

Expenditure	Previous Year	Current Year	Projected in Retirement
House			
Rent or mortgage repayments			
Water rates			
Repairs, maintenance, DIY and decoration			
Gas, electricity			
Telephone			
Household insurances			
Poll Tax			
Food and clothes			
Food and drink			
Pets			
Clothes			
Transport and travel			
Car maintenance			
Petrol and oil			
Car tax, insurance, subscriptions to AA/RAC etc			
Other travel			

Recreation
TV licence, TV rental
and video
Subscriptions
Holidays
Newspapers, periodicals etc

Personal items
Cigarettes and tobacco
Drinks and entertainment
Hairdressing
Gifts (or deeds of covenant)
Spending money
Regular savings
Life assurance
Medical insurance
Other major expenditure
Others
Total

1.2.2 Inflation

Planning ahead is not easy. But with the assistance of our Expenditure Chart it should not be impossible to estimate, however approximately, the level of income you will need when you retire.

Once you have worked out how much income you will need, it is vital to make some allowance for inflation. Obviously this is a matter of guesswork, but 5 to 10 per cent per annum would not be unrealistic. Better to over-estimate rather than underestimate. You must then ensure that your retirement income is sufficiently inflation proofed to offset the worst effects of rising prices.

It is easy to forget that even modest rates of inflation will significantly reduce the purchasing power of the pound. This can have drastic consequences for people living on fixed incomes. So bear in mind that inflation proofing is a major consideration in financial planning for retirement.

1.3 Asking yourself the right questions

This book aims to be comprehensive and therefore deals with all aspects of retirement planning. It is directed towards the middle aged as well as the elderly, and should benefit people who fit into one of the following categories:

(1) Someone planning ahead for retirement in the future:
(2) Someone about to retire who wishes to maximise post retirement income;
(3) Someone who wants to know how to pass on money and property to the family.

Let us look at the questions which should occupy each person's mind:

1   The person planning ahead

- Why are pension contributions the most tax efficient form of saving?
- What types of pension scheme are available?
- What can you do to improve the pension that you will receive from a former employer?
- Can you fund a pension for your spouse?
- What is the best way to save out of surplus income?
- What can be done at the last minute?
- How can you protect your income?

2   *The person about to retire*

- What State benefits are available?
- How can you make the most of your entitlement under company pension schemes?
- Should you take a tax free lump sum as part of your pension benefits?
- What tax will you pay after retirement?
- How can you save tax?
- What happens if you carry on working on a part-time basis?
- How can you make the most of your savings?
- What types of investment are available, how do they work, what are their pros and cons?
- How do you go about setting up a portfolio and managing your investments?
- What can you do if you have to retire on a low income?
- What are the things to consider if you want to retire abroad?
- What do you need to bear in mind if you are coming back to the UK from abroad or are a foreigner who is retiring in the UK?
- Should you pay off the mortgage?

3   *The person who is concerned about how to pass on his estate*

- What will happen if you don't make a Will?
- How should you go about making one, who should you appoint as executors etc?
- How is inheritance tax charged?
- What steps can you take to reduce the burden of this tax?

These questions are all addressed in this book.

1.4   Why is advance planning so vital?

It cannot be emphasised too strongly that life divides into two parts, your working life when you earn a salary etc, and the period after your retirement when you live off the income generated by your savings. Once you have stopped earning there will be nothing that you can do to supplement your savings, although you can of course change the way in which they are invested so as to produce additional income.

Your savings include your pension scheme and also the contributions that you have paid into the state pension scheme (these are, in effect, 'compulsory' savings). Pension schemes are the most efficient way of saving—because of the tax benefits—and hence we focus particularly on this aspect of funding your retirement income. However, there are also ways of building up your capital to supplement your post retirement income and it is important to consider these if you want to take full advantage of the opportunities that retirement provides.

You have probably given your early working years to your family, spending most of your income on housing and food (and, possibly, education of your children) now is the time to think of yourself and your spouse. Sound planning will enable you to make use of the extra free time that you will have and to do things such as travel, voluntary work, hobbies etc—all the things that the commitments of a career have prevented you from doing. If you don't plan ahead your retirement may be clouded by financial problems.

1.5   Give priority to pensions

The state benefits may be sufficient to keep the wolf from the door but even with the additional pension under the State Earnings Related Pension Scheme they are unlikely to allow you to continue your present life style, let alone expand your expenditure on those extras which make life enjoyable. If you are self-employed the state benefits are even less satisfactory because SERPS does not apply to you at all.

The sooner you start a pension scheme of your own, the better. If you and/or your employer fund your pension by making contributions at the rate of 10 per cent of your earnings and your earnings rise each year by 10 per cent, the pension will be dramatically better if you start to do this well before retirement. The following table illustrates this:

1.5.1 Table: Pension Fund Growth

Age when contributions start	Level pension as a proportion of your final earnings					
	Retirement at Age 55 Fund Growth		Retirement at Age 60 Fund Growth		Retirement at Age 65 Fund Growth	
	$8\frac{1}{2}$% pa	13% pa	$8\frac{1}{2}$% pa	13% pa	$8\frac{1}{2}$% pa	13% pa
Male aged 30 now	16.0	30.4	20.6	42.5	24.8	56.1
Female aged 30 now	14.7	28.3	18.6	39.2	22.1	50.6
Male aged 35 now	13.2	22.5	17.7	33.0	21.8	44.5
Female aged 35 now	12.1	21.0	16.0	30.4	19.3	40.1
Male aged 40 now	10.3	16.0	14.7	24.8	18.8	34.6
Female aged 40 now	9.4	14.8	18.3	22.8	16.6	31.1
Male aged 45 now	7.0	9.8	11.4	17.5	15.3	25.4
Female aged 45 now	6.4	9.1	10.4	16.1	13.6	22.9
Male aged 50 now	3.5	4.5	7.9	10.9	11.9	18.0
Female aged 50 now	3.2	4.2	7.1	10.1	10.5	16.2
Male aged 55 now	—	—	4.0	5.0	8.5	11.7
Female aged 55 now	—	—	3.6	4.6	7.7	10.7

1.5.2 Notes to table

These figures and those throughout this chapter are based on the standard rates prescribed by the Life Assurance and Unit Trust Regulatory Organisation (LAUTRO) and assume that the retirement fund built up by your contributions grows at either $8\frac{1}{2}$ per cent pa or 13 per cent pa and that your earnings increase by an average of 10 per cent per annum. The pensions are based on current LAUTRO recommended annuity rates.

It is also possible to have a pension that increases each year to help to protect your income against inflation. If you choose this option, your *starting* pension will be approximately 50 per cent of the figures shown in the table.

The figures shown are for single lives—however, if you want a pension that will continue during the liftime of yourself *and* your spouse, then you will have to settle for a lower amount.

1.6 Why are pension schemes the most tax efficient form of saving?

Most people are aware that pension plans offer one of the best means of saving for retirement. At present pension plans have three distinct advantages over other forms of long-term savings:

(1) pension funds are exempt from all UK taxes, and accordingly the fund should accumulate at a higher rate than other forms of savings
(2) at retirement part of the pension may be commuted for a tax-free lump sum
(3) up to certain limits, pension contributions attract tax relief up to the highest rate of tax.

Many self-employed people take the view that 'their business is their pension scheme'. However, this can often be shortsighted as the profitability of the business may decline if you try to continue in business when you should have retired. Furthermore, even if you are still as efficient at age 70 as you were when you were building up the business, the fact remains that the value of the business will be affected if something happens to you. How will your widow stand then?

1.7   What is the best way to save out of surplus income?

Having done all you can to maximise your pension, a further way of supplementing your retirement income is to save regularly from after-tax income in order to produce a lump sum at age 60 or 65. There are numerous schemes for just this purpose but some are not particularly tax efficient—especially if you are subject to the higher rates of income tax. Others are either tax-free or offer some tax advantage, so it is sensible to look at these first of all.

1.7.1   Endowment policies

If you are a higher rate tax payer you need a scheme that will shelter the return on your savings from the ravages of tax and there is no better arrangement than an endowment policy issued by an insurance company (often known as a 'maximum investment plan'). The income and capital growth earned by the insurance company on the money that you put into an endowment policy is taxed at life assurance company rates (25 per cent) rather than at the rates which apply to your personal income. Thus a saving scheme of this type is still treated in a favourable way for tax purposes and continues to have attractions despite the abolition of life assurance premium relief in 1984. After a certain period, the shortest being seven and a half years, you can cash in your policy and the amounts that you will then receive are totally free of tax.

1.7.2   National savings and unit trusts

There are other regular saving schemes which offer attractive returns for relatively small sums of money. Look at the National Savings yearly plan which guarantees a competitive rate of return especially to those who are liable to higher rates of tax. Up to £200 per month can be salted away under this arrangement and the return is totally tax free. Alternatively a unit trust savings plan could be most useful. This ensures a gradual build up of units and it is possible under most plans for your contributions to be spread between several different unit trusts.

1.7.3   PEPs

The Government recently introduced a further type of scheme, the 'Personal Equity Plan'. This enables you to build up a portfolio of ordinary shares and unit trusts by saving a regular sum. You can put in up to £750 per month, £9,000 per year, and your spouse can make a similar contribution.

Personal equity plans enjoy two types of tax relief. Firstly, the income within the plan is exempt from income tax. Secondly there is no capital gains tax on disposals of investments by the PEP managers. These tax incentives may seem relatively modest, but if you were to put the maximum amount into a personal equity plan for five or six, or even ten years, both the total amount invested within the plan and the tax benefits could be very substantial.

You can cash the plan in at any stage without loss of the tax benefit.

1.7.4 TESSAs

In January 1991 a new tax exempt special savings account (TESSA) became available. It will appeal to many investors as the scheme makes all interest added to the account exempt from tax provided the capital is not touched for the five year period of the plan. Savings can be made on a regular basis, or as a lump sum, up to the annual limit of £3,000 in the first year; a maximum of £1,800 can be added each year thereafter for three years, with a final sum of £600 in the fifth year, until the overall maximum of £9,000 is reached. Each spouse can have a TESSA, thus allowing £18,000 to be invested tax free by a married couple.

Regardless of which particular type of regular savings plan you use, the most important thing is to start as soon as possible. Even modest amounts saved regularly over a ten year period can produce worthwhile results. So start now at a level that you can comfortably afford and increase this as and when possible. The earlier you start the more you will accumulate. Watch the sums grow as the wonder of compound growth takes effect!

1.7.5 Example: Compound growth

A person saves £250 a year.

Number of years payments	Total sum saved	Value of savings with interest at		
		6%	8%	10%
5	£1,250	£1,493	£1,583	£1,679
10	£2,500	£3,493	£3,911	£4,382
15	£3,750	£6,168	£7,331	£8,737

It is important to remember that inflation will be eroding some of the real purchasing power of these figures, but then that is all the more reason to save wisely.

1.7.6 Tax efficient capital investments

Whereas some people will wish to create a capital sum for retirement, others may have capital which they wish to tie up in a long term tax efficient investment. In these cases, investment bonds issued by insurance companies may be attractive as the growth on a bond is not liable to income tax until such time as the investment is finally cashed in, and then is liable only to tax at the higher rate. This means in effect that you can use an investment bond to defer a tax charge. Very often people can effectively shelter investment income until after retirement at which time they may be subject to a much lower rate of tax.

1.7.7 Example: Investment bonds

(1) £10,000 invested in bonds for 10 years at (say) 8 per cent growth will be worth £21,589. Assuming tax would normally be paid at 40 per cent the liability on a bond is only 15 per cent on the gain of £11,589 (ie £1,738) and the net proceeds are then £19,851.

(2) £10,000 invested in a building society for 10 years at (say) 8 per cent net of basic rate of tax. Assuming 40 per cent tax is paid throughout the investment term the equivalent net return is approximately 6.5 per cent. Thus the net value of the investment after 10 years is £18,780. These values are approximate as the higher rate tax liability is not deducted at source and, therefore, it is difficult to calculate the exact compound rate.

This assumes that the year in which the bond is redeemed is one in which the investor is subject to the 40 per cent top rate. The bond could however be cashed in a year when tax is payable at a much lower rate. Alternatively the bond could be 'gifted' to children or grandchildren in which case they could then cash the bond without an income tax liability and thus retain the whole £21,589. This assumes that the recipient is a basic rate taxpayer.

1.7.8 Roll-up funds

Another way of deferring your taxable income and thus reducing your tax bill is to invest in an offshore 'roll-up' fund. Roll-up funds are operated by leading UK financial institutions using companies based offshore in the Isle of Man or Channel Islands. The funds themselves invest in bank deposits and very short term fixed interest investments. The income from these investments is not distributed as dividends but added to the share price, or 'rolled-up'. The funds operate in a similar way to unit trusts so that the investor realises the benefits of the accumulated income when he sells his shares. The profit is subject to income tax, but the investor can choose the year in which he has the taxable income. Very often a person can achieve an advantage by investing in a roll-up fund during his high earning years when interest would normally have attracted a higher rate of tax and then selling the shares in a year in which his taxable income is much lower. Another aspect is that whilst the capital remains invested in the roll-up fund, the money is accumulating interest often without any tax whatsoever!

1.7.9 Other savings schemes

There are many other lump sum investment schemes which also enjoy favourable tax treatment. National Saving Certificates are a good example. You may well find it worthwhile to shop around and spread your capital across a number of different investments which enjoy tax advantages.

Of course, quite apart from the taxation aspects, it can make sense to spread your investments. Tax is only one aspect and there are other considerations, such as the fact that you may need access to some of your capital in an emergency, you may want to invest some in an all-out pursuit of capital growth etc. Our section on fixed interest and capital growth investments is aimed mainly at people who have already retired and who are investing their capital but much of the detailed analysis of the way in which different types of investments work will also be of interest if you are looking ten years ahead.

1.8 Protecting your income

It is all very well formulating tax efficient savings schemes and making top up pension contributions but what can be done about protecting your income up to retirement. All the best laid plans could be wasted if you suffer long term incapacity due to illness or accident. Financial hardship could seriously reduce your capacity to pay bills or make pension contributions.

1.8.1 Income protection insurance policy

As with many risks, the answer may be to take adequate cover under an income protection insurance policy. This type of policy will normally pay you a specified income (index linked if required) while you are incapacitated, and will cease payments at a pre-selected termination date (say age 60 or 65) or on recovery whichever comes first. Provided cover is arranged at a realistic level then no serious financial consequences should result.

1.8.2   Example: typical premiums

As an example of the cost of buying such cover, a man aged 50 or 55 in good health would pay the following typical monthly premiums for cover of £100 per week, index linked, for Group A risk, terminating at age 65:

Age	13 weeks	Deferred period 26 weeks	52 weeks
	£	£	£
50	26.00	18.50	15.50
55	30.00	22.50	18.25

A similar principle can be included in many endowment and pension policies thus ensuring continuation of premium payments even if you are unable to carry on working.

1.8.3   Critical illness cover (dread disease insurance)

Until recently insurance against premature death or long term illness involved two separate policies, a life policy and a permanent health insurance.

Now it is possible to obtain the combination of life insurance and sickness cover under one policy. Termed dread disease insurance, companies will pay a claim on death or where the policyholder suffers a specified illness such as cancer or heart attack. Statistics show that middle aged people are much more likely to suffer serious illness than premature death. Critical illness policies therefore bridge a major gap in that they provide a large tax free lump sum when disability strikes.

1.8.4   Medical cover

As people grow older they inevitably need more medical attention. For this reason those who enjoy private health insurance should enquire whether they can afford to extend their private medical cover into retirement. Many are members of group schemes run by their employer and pay scant attention to this important issue, only to find that when they have retired the insurance has lapsed and they are no longer covered.

Members of a group scheme are usually allowed to switch to individual membership when they leave the service of the employer. Of course this normally entails an increase in cost as individual membership is more expensive than paying through a group scheme.

The cost is often reduced by a percentage reduction for those who decide to continue membership. BUPA for instance give a 10 per cent discount.

Age is a crucial factor. Some private medical schemes will not admit people over the age of 64. So if you wish to join or retain the insurance make sure you do not let things drift on until well past retirement. Get matters sorted out timeously or it may be too late when you realise you are uninsured.

Costs

There are a number of private health schemes and it pays to shop around if you decide that cover is for you. Look at the following schemes for example:

1.8.5 Example: private health schemes

MONTHLY COST

Insurer	Single person	Married couple
BUPA	£20.96	£41.92
PPP	£17.90	£35.80

(These premiums are applicable to people age 65.)

One scheme may seem cheaper than the other but the cover may be different. Exclusions may play a part when deciding on which scheme is the most suitable. So look carefully at the small print.

1.8.6 Tax relief

Since 6 April 1990 the government has allowed tax relief on private medical insurance premiums. To qualify for tax relief the insured must be 60 or over, but in the case of a married couple only one of them has to comply with the age rule. What is more, tax relief will usually be available to the person paying the premium. So the children of an elderly couple could gain the tax benefit if they paid for their parents' private medical insurance.

Further reading

Allied Dunbar Money Guide *Financial Planning for the Over 50s* by Robert Leach.

2 Getting assistance

Inevitably there will be people who make only very limited provision, or perhaps no provision at all, for their old age. Consequently money will be extremely tight and it may be necessary to seek assistance simply to make ends meet. While this assistance will also be of a limited amount, it will at least ensure that the basic necessities of life are provided.

State benefits can essentially be divided into two types. These are insured benefits, which are available as of right, provided you have paid the required amount of National Insurance contributions; and non-insured benefits, to which you may be entitled, but which are subject to some form of means test. In addition to the State pension scheme (including SERPS and age allowance, explained in the next chapter) the following areas of financial help from the State may be available.

2.1 State assistance

2.1.1 Income support

Income support is not available as of right, but is provided on a means tested basis. Therefore, what you get, if anything at all, will depend on your income at the time you claim. The object of income support is to ensure that you have a minimum sum on which to live after paying the mortgage (or rent) and rates, etc. For a retired couple this is around £45 per week. If your surplus income is lower than this then you could be entitled to assistance.

You can still obtain income support even if you are in receipt of State pension, part-time earnings or unemployment benefit and it is taxable in the same way.

If you get income support then you may also get free prescriptions, free NHS dental treatment and assistance with the cost of glasses.

You will not qualify for income support if you have savings of £8,000 or more. This can take the form of building society or bank deposits, National Savings Certificates, Premium Bonds or other investments. However, it does not include a car, any items of valuable furniture or jewellery.

If you believe that you can claim, then complete the claim form in leaflet SB.1. Alternatively, call at your local DSS office and discuss the matter with an official. There is also a free DSS telephone advice service. You dial the special free line 0800–666555.

The older you get the more likely it is that you will spend some time in hospital. Bear in mind that your pension will be reduced if you go into hospital for in-patient treatment on the NHS. This will happen after six weeks or immediately if you are living in a local authority home or similar place before going into hospital.

2.1.2   Housing benefit

Housing benefit is a tax-free source of assistance which is run by local councils for those on a low income. It is aimed at helping to meet the cost of rent and rates whether you own your own home or live in rented accommodation. Not all of the costs are met, only those that are essential just to live in your home. As with income support the amount of housing benefit that you receive will depend on your individual financial and personal circumstances. If you get income support and you have to pay rent and rates you will normally get the maximum in housing benefit. However, you are not necessarily ineligible for housing benefit if you are not claiming income support.

The council will ask you to provide details of your income and expenditure before granting you any assistance. They also will not be prepared to help if your savings are £8,000 or more. However, it does not depend on your National Insurance contributions.

2.1.3   The Social Fund

As the name implies, the Government has set up a fund which is to be used in the form of loans and grants. The fund is managed by the local DSS offices and is operated on a discretionary basis. If you are in receipt of income support you may be able to obtain money either as a loan or a grant. Loans of up to £1,000 are available to help people meet the cost of items such as essential furniture or household equipment. A feature of this arrangement is that the amount has to be repaid and a weekly repayment rate will be agreed and then deducted from your income support. There is also a scheme to provide crisis loans to help in the event of an emergency. Up to £1,000 can be obtained provided you qualify. Grants, by contrast, do not have to be repaid. Payments are not taxable and do not rely on National Insurance contributions.

2.2 Help for the disabled and incapacitated

The DSS pay a number of different benefits to assist people who are disabled or handicapped. The most important ones are mentioned below.

2.2.1 Mobility allowance

Mobility allowance is paid to those who cannot walk, or who walk with great difficulty. The benefit takes the form of a flat rate weekly allowance, plus an earnings related element. To qualify a person must claim for the first time before the age of 65 and be resident and living in Great Britain. Payments can continue up to the age of 80, are tax free and do not depend upon National Insurance contributions.

2.2.2 Invalidity benefit

Invalidity benefit is available where a person has been unable to work for 28 weeks as a result of illness during which he has received statutory sick pay. It is paid at the same rate as the State retirement pension (the old age pension). Payments will be made while the claimant is unable to work (except in very special circumstances) but cease at retirement. Invalidity benefit is tax free.

2.2.3 Invalidity allowance

Invalidity allowance forms part of the invalidity benefit and is payable as an extra flat rate to a claimant who is incapacitated for at least five years before state pension age. The amount of benefit can be reduced, or eliminated, where the earning related component of invalidity benefit is drawn.

2.2.4 Attendance allowance

Attendance allowance provides financial assistance to disabled people who require personal care and attention. As with other DSS benefits it is payable weekly at a flat rate, but is two tier (higher and lower rate) depending on the level of care necessary. It is tax free and does not depend on National Insurance contributions, but the claimant must be physically resident in Great Britain.

2.2.5 Invalid care allowance

Invalid care allowance is designed to give financial support to people of working age who cannot take a job because they provide more or less full time care to a disabled person. It is paid at a flat weekly rate with increases for dependants. Benefits do not depend on National Insurance contributions, but are taxable.

2.2.6 Independent Living Fund

Independent living fund was established to help pay for the costs of domestic care needed by the disabled. The amount paid can vary but more assistance is provided to those on a low income. To qualify a claimant must be living in Great Britain, receiving attendance allowance and incurring expenses to provide domestic help.

2.2.7 Government grants for home improvement

Local authorities will often help with the cost of improving a home. Assistance normally takes the form of a grant, which is not repayable. Much depends on the nature of the improvement, and grants can fall into a number of categories.

(1) Improvement grants for improvement of a property or its conversion into flats or maisonettes.
(2) Immediate grants are given automatically where a home lacks one or more 'standard amenities'.
(3) Repairs grants can be obtained to cover the cost of repair to older properties, or replace lead plumbing in houses of any age.

We all know that the subject of DSS benefits can fill a book all of its own. Financial assistance is best explored directly with the local office which will have a wide range of leaflets that explain the different benefits in detail and how to claim.

2.3 Independent organisations

Other organisations may also be able to help if you are in financial difficulties. Each will need to be contacted separately. The Citizens Advice Bureaux may be able to help. Contact your local office—they are always a useful starting point and are able to offer advice on financial matters.

Few charities provide direct assistance to elderly people who are in need of financial help. Nevertheless, organisations such as Age

Concern, and Help The Aged can give advice. The Royal United Kingdom Beneficent Association grants annuities to certain elderly persons who are impoverished or infirm. So does the Universal Beneficent Society but in this case you must be referred either by the Social Services or the DSS. You could also contact the Distressed Gentlefolk's Aid Association whose activities include the provision of emergency grants.

Some leaflets you may find helpful—available from any DSS office.

Subject	*Leaflet Number*
Which Benefit	FB2
Retirement Pensions—A guide	NP46
Retiring?	FB6
National Insurance Voluntary Contributions	N142
Your Future Pension	NP38
Help with the Community Charge	CCB1
Housing Benefit—Help with Rent	RR1
Housing Benefit and Community Charge Benefit—A guide	RR2
Income Support—A guide	IS20
Income Support—Cash help	IS1
Invalidity Benefit	N116A
Sick or disabled	FB28
Social Fund—A guide	SB16
Unemployment Benefit and your occupational pension	N1230
Going into hospital	N19

Further reading

Allied Dunbar Money Guide *Financial Care For Your Elderly Relatives* by Beverly Chandler.

3 Planning your pension

Most people when they retire become entitled to a number of different pensions. To begin with there is the state basic retirement pension, in addition to which there may well be benefits from the state earnings related scheme. On top of these, it is likely in many cases that the individual will also be entitled to a pension from his employer's pension scheme, or from a personal pension plan in the case of those who were either in non-pensionable employment or who were self-employed.

This chapter sets out the position regarding your pension benefits and describes some of the alternatives that you may encounter.

3.1 State pensions

The starting point for anyone concerned about his income in retirement must be to establish exactly what pension can be expected from the state. There is some confusion in the minds of many people about this subject because of all the changes that have taken place in the past.

At present the State retirement pension can be divided into two parts.

3.1.1 Basic retirement pension

The basic retirement pension is applicable to everybody whether employed or self-employed. At the time of writing, this is £52.00 per week for a single person and £83.25 per week for a married couple. This is raised by the Government in line with the Retail Price Index in April of each year.

To qualify for the full amount you must be 65 (for a man) or 60 (for a woman) and have paid sufficient National Insurance contributions during your working life; this is defined as paying contributions for about 90 per cent of your working life between the ages of 16 and 65 (or 60 for women). For those who have not satisfied these conditions, a reduced pension will be paid. You should receive a pension claim form from the Department of Social Security about four months before you retire and if you do not receive this, then you should make enquiries at your local DSS office.

If you are a married woman and your husband is still working, a pension can still be claimed at the rate applicable to the single person provided you are aged 60 and you have paid enough National Insurance contributions in your own right. If you satisfy the contribution conditions only in part, you may get a lower rate. When your husband retires you can then claim the full married woman's rate (£31.25) if this is higher. Where a married woman has not paid sufficient contributions to earn her own pension then she must wait until her husband retires. Then she can claim a pension based on her husband's contributions. A degree of care must be exercised in this regard, as there are a number of alternatives available and the choice of pension will depend on individual circumstances.

In order to qualify for the maximum basic retirement pension (the Old Age Pension) you must satisfy the contribution conditions. Why not obtain a forecast of your pension from the DSS (complete form RR19) which will tell you whether you are entitled to the full pension? If you are not, then it may be possible to bring the contributions up to the desired level by paying voluntary contributions (Class 3). Do this as soon as possible. Once a man reaches age 65 and a woman 60, they can no longer pay contributions for back years.

Graduated pension

Before the state earnings related pension scheme was introduced, there was another scheme in force known as the state graduated pension scheme. You may be entitled to some benefits from this in addition to the state earnings related pension, but the extra amount is not significant.

3.1.2   State Earnings Related Pension Scheme

The state earnings related scheme was introduced in 1978. It is intended to improve the position of employees who are not in a company pension scheme and to provide an earnings related pension which will be payable in addition to the basic state pension.

The amount that you get depends upon your middle-tier earnings and the date when you retire. Because the earnings limit is relatively low, the maximum pension from this source is unlikely to be sufficient for a comfortable retirement.

On the other hand, SERPS is index-linked so that the pension is increased each year in line with inflation and this can make it a most valuable benefit even given the fact that no-one who retires at present is entitled to the full pension.

In 1991/92 middle tier earnings are those falling between £52.00 and £390.00 per week. Each year's earnings are revalued annually until normal retirement in line with movements in national average earnings. In consequence, a person retiring in April 1991 whose earnings have exceeded middle tier earnings throughout the scheme will be entitled to receive an additional pension of approximately £48.00 per week on the current basis. The basis of calculation changed from 1988 and, as a result, SERPS pensions will reduce once the new historical earnings basis takes effect.

At present a widow may inherit the whole of her husband's earnings related pension but this entitlement will eventually be reduced to 50 per cent. This change will, however, not take place until the year 2000.

The scheme does not affect everyone. In order to benefit from SERPS you must be 'contracted in' which means that you and your employer pay higher National Insurance contributions. If you work for an employer then you will be in SERPS unless you have been 'contracted out'. Most contracted out schemes are on a 'final salary' basis (eg so many sixtieths or eightieths depending upon length of service). These types of schemes mean that company pension schemes will be at least as good as SERPS. It is possible, however, to be a member of SERPS *and* a member of a company pension scheme and this is particularly beneficial where you have earnings in excess of the 'upper earnings limit'. It will also mean that you can fund for the maximum pension of two thirds salary in addition to your SERPS pension.

State pensions are useful because they are linked to the cost of living or to earnings and will retain their value. The basic retirement pension makes a significant contribution to either a single person's or a married couple's budget and the state earnings related pension already provides a useful addition to this. In a few more years it will be much more important.

3.1.3   Self-employed persons

Those who are self-employed cannot be eligible for SERPS and therefore will qualify only for the basic state retirement pension.

3.2   Occupational or company pension schemes

Company or 'private' pension schemes operated by your employer are also sometimes called 'occupational' pension schemes. The benefits under such schemes can vary considerably: one problem is that for many years the emphasis in the legislation was on making sure that the benefits provided were not too generous. Legislation requiring *minimum* benefits is a relatively recent thing whereas all schemes have to comply with limits laid down by the Inland Revenue.

The maximum pension permitted by the Inland Revenue is two thirds of your 'final remuneration' ie salary and other taxable earnings at the date of retirement. This can be provided to anyone who has achieved twenty years service but it is very rare for a company scheme to be as generous as this. In practice most schemes provide a pension of one sixtieth of final salary for each year of service. This provides the maximum pension of two thirds final salary for a person who has worked with the company for 40 years. Some schemes provide even less. It is, however, increasingly common for additional benefits to be given to senior staff who have joined late in their career.

The definition of final remuneration is often complex in order to protect a person whose earnings suffer a fall in the last year or two of his working life. If you are anxious to compare the details of the scheme to which you belong with others, there is the *Allied Dunbar Pensions Guide* which covers the subject.

The most important thing to do is to establish exactly what benefits you will get under your company scheme and this can best be done by consulting your employer. So as a first step you should compare your expected pension to the maximum that the Inland Revenue will permit you to have. If there is any shortfall, then think about ways to top it up.

About half the people who work for companies belong to occupational pension schemes as well as the state pension scheme. Some company schemes are contracted out of SERPS, whereas others operate on top of it. If the company scheme is contracted out you will not receive an earnings related pension from the state so your company pension ought to be at least equal to what SERPS would have produced.

3.3 Topping up a company pension scheme

3.3.1 Additional voluntary contributions

As we have said, it is in fact quite rare for a person to be entitled to as much from a pension scheme as the Inland Revenue would allow him to have; if you are not so entitled, you should take every opportunity to improve your pension. Why not make use of a scheme which permits you to pay money as additional voluntary contributions to improve your pension? All employers have these additional voluntary contributions (AVC) schemes, some are linked to building society investment, while others are operated through insurance companies. You may also make contributions to an AVC scheme of your own which is separate from your employer's Scheme. This is called a Free Standing AVC (FSAVC).

Everyone is free to contribute up to 15 per cent of his or her income towards a pension scheme and claim full tax relief (up to Revenue limits). In practice, few pension schemes require obligatory contributions on anything like this scale. So the difference between the five per cent or six per cent which you may be obliged to contribute to the main pension scheme and the full 15 per cent entitlement can be paid into an AVC scheme. Not only is full tax relief available on these contributions, but the funds accumulate free of UK tax until retirement. At that time they can be drawn, together with any other pension entitlement.

Up to 7 April 1987, AVC's could be used to accumulate a cash sum and, provided this fell within the allowances, the whole amount could be taken tax free. This was far more effective than any other means of regular saving. Until 1984, a regular saver could save through a life assurance policy and obtain a measure of tax relief on the premiums. However, this relief only amounted to half the basic rate of tax and in any event the relief is not available in respect of policies taken out after 13 March 1984. Nevertheless, anyone entered into an AVC prior to 7 April 1987 can top it up to the full 15 per cent and still take the proceeds in cash.

Under an FSAVC scheme a person obtains basic rate tax relief at source. This reduces the initial cost and in the case of a higher rate taxpayer higher tax can be claimed through the tax assessment. In addition, the growth within the fund is free from income tax and capital gains tax which will obviously produce a much better result than a comparable investment that is subject to tax.

3.3.2   Salary sacrifice

A salary sacrifice arrangement is one where an individual gives up some of his salary, with the amount that has been given up being paid by the employer into an approved pension scheme. Income tax relief is obtained at the individual's top rate because the amount given up no longer forms part of his taxable income. Salary sacrifice arrangements are especially attractive for the high income earner. There can also be a useful saving in the employer's National Insurance contributions because the company saves up to 10.45 per cent of the amount given up by the employee. This saving to the employer may enable an increase to be made in the employer's contributions. It is also possible to sacrifice bonus payments to achieve the same result.

A salary sacrifice requires the agreement of both the company and the employee and must be properly documented in order to obtain Inland Revenue approval. Provided the right procedures are followed, the advantages are considerable, especially for those who would not otherwise receive an adequate company pension.

3.3.3   Choosing the level of payment

When members of pension schemes retire they are usually given a choice of how they wish the income to be paid. It is possible to have a pension which will only continue for as long as one person survives. Alternatively, they can choose a smaller pension which will continue throughout the life of both husband and wife (known as joint life pension). The size of the reduction depends upon their ages. If they are both 65, a fund of £10,000 could provide them with a lifetime income of, for example, around £1,200 per year. For the same fund a single man of 65 could expect aroun £1,500 a year.

The exact pension would, of course, depend on rates available in the market at retirement.

The choice of the appropriate type of pension depends upon individual circumstances. A popular choice for married couples is a joint life pension which reduces to a lower amount after the first death. This protects the survivor but recognises the fact that one can live more cheaply than two.

3.3.4 Commuting company pension for cash

It is normal for a person at retirement to be given the option of exchanging part of the pension for a tax-free lump sum. This is a valuable benefit but many people are not sure whether it is really to their advantage to cash in their pension and have difficulty making up their minds whether or not to take advantage of the opportunity.

At first sight, the choice between a tax-free sum now and taxable pension seems straightforward. Even if you do not need the lump sum now, it seems more sensible to take it. This may, however, be an over-simplification and some people may be better off with the pension.

The Inland Revenue restricts the size of the tax-free lump sum which can be given. The maximum allowed is one and a half times a person's final remuneration (including benefits in kind), but smaller amounts may be given depending on the actual length of service. The most critical question is how much pension must be sacrificed in return for the lump sum. There is a table of factors which has been agreed among the insurance companies and the faculty of actuaries:

3.3.5 Example: actuarial factors

LEVEL PENSION

	Age	*Factor*
Men	60	10.2
	65	9.0
	70	7.8
Women	55	12.2
	60	11.0
	65	9.8

The factors for other ages can be calculated by an increase or decrease of 0.02 per month of age. In order to calculate the reduction in pension, the lump sum should be divided by it.

Thus, a woman retiring at 60 and receiving a tax-free lump sum of £11,000 would have her pension reduced by £1,000 per annum. A pension scheme does not have to use these factors and can choose others which are more or less favourable.

3.3.6   Is commuting pensions worthwhile?

Let us look at the position of a man of 65 who commutes £2,000 worth of pension (£1,500 after tax of 25 per cent) for a cash sum of £18,000. He can invest this money in a purchased life annuity from a life company. Let us assume this produces a gross income of £2,800 pa. £1,260 of it will be tax-free, (known as the capital content) leaving only £1,540 taxable. This gives a net income after basic rate tax of £2,415 in contrast to £1,500 from the pension. By taking the cash sum and reinvesting it, the net income after tax has increased by £915.

3.3.7   Pensions and inflation

Our example is a perfectly valid comparison if the pension from the company scheme is properly comparable to the annuity which has been bought from the insurance company. However, the two will not always be comparable because a great many superannuation schemes will increase pensions in course of payment. Insurance companies do not do this for annuities unless it is part of the contract.

This factor can make it difficult to compare the benefit of giving up pension for a cash sum. If inflation revives and the pension scheme increases the benefit in payment to match it, the income payable will soon overtake any annuity which can be purchased for the cash sum. On the other hand, inflation may continue to decline and even if it does not, the pension scheme may not keep pace with it.

Pensions in the public sector normally match inflation, but few private ones do this. However, a high proportion of the major employers in the private sector make discretionary increases to pensions in payment and in recent years these have tended to match inflation.

There are a few company pension schemes in which the pension increases automatically after retirement. When this is the case, the commutation value of the pension will be different. In effect you will get more cash for each pound of pension surrendered.

The best way of assessing your own position is to find out the record of your employer over the last few years. If there is no contractual obligation on the company to continue making increases, there is a strong moral one. If pensions have kept pace with the cost of living in the past then it is likely that they will do so in the future. If they have not done so, then you should not expect them to in the future unless you have clear evidence of a change of heart. In the absence of any increase it is clearly to your advantage to take the cash sum. If, on the other hand, you can expect a pension which will more or less keep pace with inflation the decision is much more finely balanced.

Of course, investment considerations are not the only ones. If the pension you will receive is more than sufficient after commuting a portion and you have uses for the cash you should of course take it. The fact remains that many people find that as retirement approaches they have more than sufficient cash and when this is the case they can simply choose the most financially advantageous arrangement.

3.4 Personal pension schemes

If you do not belong to a company pension scheme or if you are self-employed then you may arrange a personal pension scheme. Unlike a company scheme member, it is the amount you may contribute which is laid down by the Inland Revenue (as opposed to Final Benefits limits on company schemes). At the present time the limits are as follows:

Age on 6 April	*Percentage*
35 or less	17.5%
36 to 45	20.0%
46 to 50	25.0%
51 to 55	30.0%
56 to 60	35.0%
61 and over	40.0%

These percentages apply to 'net relevant earnings' which can be broadly defined as earnings from your non-pensionable employment or business, less certain deductions such as expenses, trading losses, capital allowances etc.

If you are in a position of having two sources of income, one from pensionable employment and the other being net relevant earnings, you may contribute up to the above limit in respect of your net relevant earnings regardless of the level of your pensionable earnings. So you can have two pensions, one provided by your employer and the other provided by you out of your own pocket.

In addition to the above limits, you are also allowed to make a contribution in respect of unpaid contributions during the previous six years. Thus for those making their first personal pension contributions in the 1991/92 tax year, an additional sum may also be paid in respect of 1985/86 and subsequent years. As a means of providing for retirement this is an especially useful allowance.

If you wish to gain the maximum benefit from your pension contributions then the sooner they are paid the better. The following table illustrates this point vividly.

As the figures show, a delay of five years in starting a pension is expensive and may also cause a considerable burden in later years as an effort is made to make up for the lost time. Any insurance company, actuary or other qualified adviser will strongly recommend that you start a pension plan as soon as you can afford to do so.

3.4.1   Table: Personal pension schemes

Annual level pension contribution £1,000 (£750 net of relief at 25%)

Male	*Estimated pension fund at age 60*	
Age next birthday	*Fund growth of $8\frac{1}{2}$% pa*	*Fund growth of 13% pa*
	£	£
35	72,900	143,000
40	45,400	75,800
45	26,900	38,800
50	14,400	18,100

3.4.2   Commuting personal pension plans

Where you have paid personal pension premiums, ie you have contributed to a personal pension scheme unconnected to an employer, then commutation is a reasonably straightforward matter. Current legislation allows the insurance company to pay a tax-free lump sum which of course requires the surrender of part of the pension entitlement. However, in most cases it is advantageous to take the cash and reinvest in a purchased life annuity, with its tax-free 'capital content' as described above. This feature, therefore, restricts the tax charge to only the interest element of the annuity and accordingly the after tax income is higher than it would be from the pension which is wholly taxable.

3.4.3   A personal pension or SERPS?

Are you under 50? If you are then what follows may be of great interest. Since 1 July 1988 it has been possible to contract out of the state earning related pension scheme (SERPS) by taking out one of the new Appropriate Personal Pension (APP) plans. This concession applies irrespective of whether the employee is a member of an occupational pension scheme (provided that scheme is not already contracted out). Clearly this is an important development as it offers contracting out to a large number of employees who had previously had no choice but to contribute to SERPS. A full description of SERPS can be found on page 24 and this should be read in conjunction with this section.

3.4.4 Paying for contracting out

When contracting out, SERPS is replaced by a rebate of National Insurance contributions applied to 'band earning'. For the 1991/92 tax year the rebate is 5.8 per cent and 'band earnings' are £52.00 to £390.00 per week. The employee's share of the rebate (two per cent) attracts tax relief and so, grossed up by 25 per cent, this increases to 2.67 per cent. On top of that there is an additional two per cent incentive for two years in respect of those contracting out for the first time. This is to encourage contracting out. Cumulatively the rebate will be 8.47 per cent for the current tax year.

Contracting out through personal pensions was possible from 6 April 1987. However, as Personal Pensions were not introduced until July 1988 the Government allowed back-dating to the 1987/88 fiscal year. For that year the cumulative rebate is 9.05 per cent.

The mechanics

Once a decision has been made to contract out, the first step is to choose the pension provider. Normally this will be issued through an insurance company, although other financial institutions can now issue personal pension schemes. To establish a policy an Application to the pension provider must be made together with a Joint Notice. The DSS will be notified of the amount of the NIC paid by the employer via the Inland Revenue returns submitted by the employer after the end of the tax year. It will then calculate the rebate and pay this to the pensions provider who will invest the money in its pension fund on behalf of the employee.

Who will benefit

While the opportunity to contract out extends to all members of SERPS, it is by no means beneficial for everyone to do so. There is an important difference between SERPS and a personal pension. Under SERPS the Government will guarantee to pay a defined amount of pension (depending on age and earnings). By contrast, the personal pension contains few, if any, guarantees and the eventual pension depends upon investment returns during the life of the policy. Using reasonable assumptions, it could be advantageous for males 50 and under and females under 45 to contract out.

Conclusions

Undoubtedly many employees should consider contracting out with Appropriate Personal Pensions. This is, however, a somewhat complex topic on which expert advice should be sought.

3.4.5   Self-employed pensions

Self-employed people pay a lower rate of national insurance contributions than the combined employer's/employee's contributions. This is one of the several fiscal benefits enjoyed by self-employed people. If you simply put the difference or 'saving', into a personal pension play you could build up significant benefits.

3.4.6   Example: self-employed pensions

A makes profits of £30,000. If he carried on the business through a company and took out a salary of £30,000 the following amounts would be payable as National Insurance Contributions:

Payable by A personally	£1,636
Payable by company	£3,135
	£4,771

As A is self-employed the maximum payable for 1991/92 is £1,178.89 (Class ii £272.95, Class iv £905.94 the latter being 50 per cent tax deductible).

Thus A could afford to put away private pension contributions of £3,500 and still be no worse off than if he had carried on his business through a company. Paying index linked contributions at this rate from age 40 would produce a substantial pension—according to standard LAUTRO assumptions the pension available at age 65 would represent between 15 per cent and 44 per cent of final earnings, assuming actual growth was between the two LAUTRO growth rates of 8½ per cent and 13 per cent pa and that salary rose by 10 per cent pa.

3.4.7   Pensions from former employers

It is well known that people who have changed jobs ('early leavers') often lose out in terms of pension. As a general practice, the most that an early leaver used to be able to expect was a frozen pension and this could have very unfair results.

3.4.8 Example: early leaver's pension

A has done 40 years service with one company. He retires on a final salary of £24,000. He might well receive a pension of 40/60 × 24,000, ie £16,000.

B worked for 20 years with one company and his salary on leaving amounted to £5,000. He then worked for the same company as A and retired on a salary of £30,000. B's pension income is likely to be made up of two parts:

pension from first employer

20/60 × salary on leaving of £5,000   1,667

pension from second employer

20/60 × final salary of £30,000   10,000
          11,667

Whereas A gets a pension of nearly 67 per cent of his final earnings, B gets pensions which amount to only 39 per cent of his final salary.

Recent legislation has improved the position for the early leaver, but you should carefully explore your pension position if you decide to change jobs of if you have changed jobs in the past.

3.4.9 Transfer values

One way to reduce this problem is to arrange for a transfer value to be paid from the trustees of your former employer's pension scheme into your new pension scheme. However, the terms have to be negotiated between the actuaries involved and you may find that a transfer value which reflects the value of your future benefits in respect of (say) 10 years past service buys the equivalent of only (say) six years benefits under your new scheme. This is very much an area where you need professional advice.

3.4.10 Buy-out bonds

Another option which is now available as of right in respect of some pre 1985 service is to arrange for the trustees of your former employer's pension scheme to purchase a deferred annuity contract under the provisions of ICTA 1988, s 591. These 'buy-out' or so-called 'section 32' bonds may offer better value than a transfer value—but once again you should obtain professional advice on the implications in your particular situation.

3.4.11   Portable pensions

'Portable' pensions are what the public wants and the Government has passed legislation to remove barriers to this. It is now possible to transfer benefits from an occupational scheme to a personal pension scheme (this type of policy is normally only available to those in non pensionable employment). This could be an attractive alternative to the buy-out bond as the proceeds can be taken from age 50 and usually up to 25 per cent of final fund can be taken in cash.

3.5   What benefits are available?

Finally, when everything else has been done, it is important to ensure that you will obtain the best possible benefits.

3.5.1   Open market options

Certain types of pension scheme offer what is known as an open market option. This enables a person to 'shop around' at the time of his retirement and use the funds which he has accumulated with one insurance company to buy an annuity from another if their rates are better at that time. In practice, there are considerable differences in annuity rates and it is well worth looking around to ensure that the annuity quoted by your own insurance company is the best available.

As an indication of the amount of variation, the rates quoted by two insurance companies for a single life annuity for a man aged 65 and a fund of £10,000 varied from £1,477 to £1,530 per annum.

It should be noted that some insurance companies impose a 'transfer fee' or charge where a fund is transferred to another insurance company. Other companies give a 'loyalty bonus', ie the normal annuity rates are enhanced for people who have had a pension contract with the company concerned. Even so, it is still well worth obtaining competitive quotations (if an open market option forms part of your pension arrangements).

3.5.2   Widow's pension

When deciding on the type of pension that most suits your requirements, bear in mind that under the state scheme the widow's pension is limited to the amount payable to a single person (provided she is widowed after age 60). This boils down to the basic retirement pension for a single person plus the amount payable under the earnings related scheme. Therefore it may well be advisable to choose a *lower* pension that continues during the lifetime of your widow.

3.5.3 Invalidity benefit

If you are drawing invalidity benefit when you reach age 65 (if you are a man) or 60 (if you are female) you must decide whether you wish to continue to do so for a further five years, or elect to take the basic retirement pension instead. In some cases this may not be a straightforward matter because these two benefits are not treated in the same way by the Inland Revenue.

Since November 1980, invalidity benefit has not been subject to income tax whereas state pensions are fully taxable. So this presents a problem and the choice will depend on the amount of income you will enjoy apart from either the invalidity benefit or state pension. To resolve the matter, add up all your other gross income (that is the amount before tax is taken off) such as private pensions, building society interest, etc. If the total of these items is greater than your personal allowance then you should retain the invalidity benefit. This will save you paying the extra tax that would arise if you decide to draw the basic retirement pension.

3.6 Can you fund a pension for your wife?

Many business and professional people employ their wives, mainly on a part-time basis where the salary is insufficient to attract income tax and National Insurance contributions. Where this happens, and provided the main income is taxed under Schedule D, it is possible to arrange a pension scheme for the wife who is technically an employee. There are four significant advantages in doing so; the first three may be obvious but the fourth will not.

Firstly, the contributions paid into the pension scheme are treated as a business expense and thus qualify for tax relief. Second, there is the attraction of investing money in a tax exempt fund. Third, a pension scheme may be an effective 'tax shelter' for those who pay tax at the higher rates because the pension shelters the growth on the contributions and repays them with the interest when your tax liabilities are lower. Fourth, when the pension is paid to the wife it qualifies for treatment as earned income in her hands. This means that the wife's personal allowance is offset against the pension and thus a significant amount of the income will not suffer tax. Also remember that there will be the right to take out a tax free cash sum.

It may well be that the salary involved is low and you may think that such an arrangement would not be worthwhile. This is certainly not so. As we explained in 3.2, the maximum pension that an employee can receive at retirement is two thirds of salary at that time. In order to ensure that people are not unduly restricted in terms of their pension contributions, the Inland Revenue will allow the employee's present-day salary to be increased by 8.5 per cent per year to their normal retirement date, and approve contributions that will fund a pension of up to two thirds of that sum. Thus it is possible for worthwhile amounts to be paid even though the current salary appears not to justify them. In many cases putting money into a pension scheme on behalf of your spouse is more tax efficient than paying contributions for yourself.

3.6.1 Example: funding a wife's pension

Husband age 50 employs his wife age 48 on a salary of £1,800 a year.

The current salary of £1,800 is assumed to increase by $8\frac{1}{2}\%$ a year to age 60, making a pensionable salary of approximately £4,700.

Pension can be provided to $\frac{2}{3}$ of £4,700 (say)	£3,100
Level pension premium of £90.00 per month paid by husband produces a pension fund at age 60	£19,800 (at $8\frac{1}{2}\%$ pa)
	£26,200 (at 13% pa)
After tax relief at 25 per cent the husband pays out total contributions of	£9,720.00
Wife receives—tax free cash sum (assuming no past service) of	£2,510
plus lifetime level pension of	£1,580 (at $8\frac{1}{2}\%$ pa)
	£2,520 (at 13% pa)

As the pension is less than the wife's personal allowance, there is no income tax to pay on the pension. So you get the unbeatable combination of tax relief on your savings, investment in a tax free fund, a tax free lump sum at retirement plus an income on which you do not have to pay tax.

Under the new personal pension regulations it is now possible for non taxpayers in receipt of earned income to provide themselves with a pension and get tax relief on the premium.

As with tax relief on mortgage interest, non taxpayers can deduct tax at the basic rate from their contribution before paying it over to the insurance company. To qualify, you must be in employment (not self employment). This concession allows people on modest incomes (often wives who work part time) to contribute to their own pension scheme.

3.6.2 Example: non taxpayer's pension

Mrs A earns £2,500 as a part time secretary. Because she is 50 she can pay up to 25 per cent of her earnings into a personal pension policy. If she were to retire at age 60, the benefits might be as follows:

	£
Monthly gross contribution	50.00
Tax relief at 25%	12.50
Net amount paid	37.50
Total amount paid to retirement	4,312.50

	$8\frac{1}{2}$% growth	13% growth
At age 60 she could draw		
Tax free cash	£1,950	£2,430
Pension for life	£542 per year	£780 per year

Again there is the combination of tax relief on savings, tax free growth and tax free income.

3.7 What can be done at the last minute?

When a person draws near to his retirement date it is worth considering whether additional voluntary contributions or personal pension contributions can be paid. Even though the money may be with the insurance company for a relatively short time, the fact that the contributions attract income tax relief and a lump sum may be taken tax-free means that there is often substantial advantage in paying such contributions. Here are two typical examples to illustrate the possible benefits:

3.7.1 Example: woman of 59

A woman approaching 60 decided to pay a personal pension contribution. A single payment of £1,000 would attract 25 per cent income tax relief and so the net cost would be only £750. If she took the benefits six months later she might expect to receive a tax-free lump sum of £276 ($8\frac{1}{2}$ per cent pa growth) or £293 (13 per cent pa growth) plus an on-going pension of £78 pa ($8\frac{1}{2}$ per cent pa growth) or £96 pa (13 per cent pa growth).

The benefits can be even greater for a person who is subject to tax at the maximum rate of 40 per cent.

3.7.2   Example: man of 64

A man aged 64 is due to retire on his 65th birthday in three months' time. If he pays £5,000 personal pension premiums the following position is likely to obtain:

Personal pension premium	£5,000
less tax relief at 40%	£2,000
	£3,000
less 25% tax free lump sum on retirement	£1,250
Net cost	£1,750

In return for this net outlay, he could expect to receive an on-going pension of £562 (at $8\frac{1}{2}$ per cent pa) or £638 (at 13 per cent pa) or less if benefits are to be provided for widow.

Don't forget that you can pay personal pension premiums if you have non-pensionable earnings even though you may also have pensionable earnings from another employment.

Further reading

Allied Dunbar Pensions Guide by Tony Reardon.
Allied Dunbar Money Guide *Planning Your Pension* by Tony Reardon.

4   Going early, going late

Nowadays more people are retiring before attaining official pension age (65 for a man and 60 for a woman). This can occur for a number of reasons, such as redundancy, illness or perhaps because the desire to work is not as strong as it once was. Whatever the reason, it is well to be aware of the implications as far as state benefits are concerned.

4.1   Early retirement

No one can draw state pension before the official pension age. Nevertheless if you are a member of an occupational pension scheme it may be possible for a male to draw pension benefits from age 50 (45 for females) provided they are within 10 years of their normal retirement date. This may well cause their benefits to be reduced but nevertheless at least the option exists. Where retirement is on grounds of ill health the benefits from the scheme can be calculated as though they had retired normally, but their final salary must be that at the date of early retirement. Self-employed people and those in non-pensionable employment must look to their personal pension schemes for retirement income. Under retirement annuity policies, it is not possible to draw benefits before age 60 unless retirement is the result of ill health. However, with the introduction in July 1988 of personal pension schemes, with their early retirement age of 50, all this has now changed. The Inland Revenue will sanction the transfer of a pension fund from a retirement annuity policy to a personal pension under which benefits can be drawn at any time after age 50. By this means the self-employed can now enjoy the fruits of their savings much earlier.

A factor to consider is the impact early retirement may have on the basic retirement pension. Whether you are an employee or you are self-employed, early retirement could affect your entitlement because to draw the maximum basic pension you must have a full contribution record. By cutting short your working life your NI contributions may be insufficient to entitle you to the full pension. In these circumstances it is as well to check with your social security office that you have paid enough contributions. If your contributions are deficient you can pay voluntary contributions (Class 3) to ensure that you are entitled to the full pension when you get to age 65 (male) or 60 (female).

4.1.1   Unemployment

If you are early retired you can still register as unemployed and apply for benefit, subject to satisfactory National Insurance contributions. To qualify, it is a condition that you are capable of and available for work, and you may be penalised if you refuse to accept or apply for any reasonable offer of work. By registering as unemployed you can obtain a credit towards the basic retirement pension and this will ensure you do not lose out when it is eventually drawn.

Unemployment benefit is £41.40 per week with an extra £25.55 for a wife. The rates are increased for those over pensionable age to £52.00 and £31.25 respectively. If compulsory redundancy has occurred then the benefit is payable immediately, but if it was voluntary then it is deferred for up to 26 weeks. However, anyone aged 55 or over and in receipt of an occupational pension of more than £35.00 per week will have their unemployment benefit reduced by 10p for every 10p that exceeds £35.

4.1.2   Sickness benefits

People who fall ill or become disabled while unemployed should be able to claim state sickness benefit instead of unemployment benefit. The advantage is that currently unemployment benefit is taxable but sickness benefit is not.

Sickness benefit is payable for 28 weeks and after that they may be able to claim invalidity benefit which enjoys the same non-taxable status.

4.2   Carry on working—part time work

Naturally, whereas some people are keen to retire early others are reluctant to give up work completely and choose to continue on a part-time basis. This raises several questions:

- How much can you earn without affecting your state pension?
- What happens if you defer taking your state pension?

- What happens if you do not draw your company pension right away?
- How will your part-time earnings be assessed for tax purposes and what is the National Insurance position?
- What can you do to save tax?

4.2.1   How much can you earn without affecting your state pension?

Working on a part-time basis after age 65 will not result in a restriction of the state pension. Where a husband is retired but has a working wife under the age of 60 he can claim the £31.25 per week extra pension for her. However, if she earns more than £41.40 a week (including any occupational pension) then the extra pension will stop. Once she attains the age of 60 and draws a pension in her own right then the reduction in the pension will come to an end.

4.2.2   What happens if you defer taking your state pension?

It may be that if you are working, say, three days a week, that you can afford to defer drawing your pension. This may enable the pension to be increased substantially when you eventually start to take it. The state pension can, in fact, be deferred until age 70. Deferring the pension results in its being increased by approximately seven and a half per cent per annum. Over five years this means that the pension is increased by a third—in addition to any inflation adjustments.

4.2.3   What happens if you do not draw your company pension right away?

In some cases, especially where you have an executive pension scheme (sometimes known as an individual pension arrangement) it is possible to defer taking the pension and this can be a sensible way to proceed because of the tax free nature of the pension fund.

Similarly, if you have made additional voluntary contributions you may be able to draw the benefits under the main pension scheme but defer the benefits funded under the AVC scheme.

Unfortunately, if you are a member of the large group scheme there is often less scope for manoeuvre. It may be that the choices open to you are simply either to retire and start drawing your pension or to carry on working. This is something that you should investigate, probably via your company's personnel department.

4.2.4 How will your part-time earnings be assessed for tax purposes?

The position will vary according to whether you are employed or self-employed. This will normally depend upon whether you are working on a part-time basis for a single employer or are working on a freelance basis for several different customers—although other considerations may also be relevant. In some cases the distinction may be difficult to draw and you would be well advised to obtain a copy of the Inland Revenue leaflet *Employed or self-employed?*

If you are employed then your earnings will be taxed under the PAYE system. You may well have your code number amended to reflect the fact that you are drawing your state pension. Your taxable earnings will be those which arise during the year. There are very few allowable expenses.

If you are self-employed your taxable earnings will normally be assessed on the 'preceding year' basis. This is the normal basis of assessment for a self-employed person and means that the income for a tax year is taken to be the profits of his accounts which end in the preceding tax year.

4.2.5 Example: preceding year basis of accounts

A draws up his accounts to 30 June. His profits for the year ended 30 June 1991 will determine the tax assessment for 1992/93.

4.2.6 Starting a new business

A special rule applies when a person starts a new business. His profits for the first year are based upon his actual earnings from the date he commenced his business to the following 5 April. For the second tax year he is assessed on his earnings for the first 12 months of trading.

4.2.7 Example: a new business

A starts a business on 1 January 1991 with an accounting year end 31 December 1991

His results are as follows:

Year ended 31 December 1991	£6,000
Year ended 31 December 1992	£12,000
Year ended 31 December 1993	£15,000

The tax assessments would be:

1990/91 3/12 × £6,000 (ie profits from 1.1.91 to 5.4.91)	£1,500
1991/92 First 12 months	£6,000
1992/93 Preceding year basis	£6,000
1993/94 Preceding year basis	£12,000

The basis of assessment suits A here as he is assessed on a total of £13,500 whereas his actual earnings for the period amounted to £33,000! However, if it had been the other way round A could elect for his tax assessments for his second and third year and to be based on his actual profits. Note that the election can only be made by the taxpayer and that it cannot be made for one year in isolation.

Note also that there are closing year rules for when business ceases and this could mean a heavier tax liability to counterbalance the lower liability in the opening year.

4.2.8   National Insurance contributions

National Insurance contributions will not be payable by you after age 65 (60 for women) but if you are employed your employer may still be liable for contributions.

4.2.9   How can you save tax?

The rules on what expenses are allowable are much easier if you are self-employed—especially if you work from home. An employed person has to show that expenses have been incurred 'wholly, exclusively and necessarily' in performing the duties of the employment. A self-employed person need only show that they were incurred 'wholly and exclusively' for business purposes. You should for example be able to claim for:

- Travelling expenses (not to and from your office to home)
- Postage and stationery
- Telephone, heat and light

and possibly a payment to your wife for secretarial work.

These are things which you should discuss with an accountant, together with matters such as:

- Can you claim expenses for using part of your home for business purposes?

- What other expenses will be allowable?
- Will you need to register for VAT purposes?

There are two other tax planning points which are worthy of special mention: choosing the right accounting date and paying private pension contributions.

One idea is to draw up accounts to 30 April so as to take full advantage of the preceding year basis (this assumes that profits will be increasing year by year).

4.2.10   Example: choosing the right accounting date

B starts a business on 1 January 1988. His first accounts are for a period of one year and four months, ie up to 30 April 1989. Suppose his actual profits are:

First 16 months	£8,000
Year to 30 April 1990	10,000
Year to 30 April 1991	12,000
Year to 30 April 1992	15,000
	45,000

His taxable income may well be much less and will usually be worked out as follows:

1987/88	3/16 × £8,000 (ie profits to 5.4.87)	£1,500
1988/89	12/16 × £8,000 (ie first twelve months profits)	6,000
1989/90	12/16 × £8,000 (ie next twelve months profits)	6,000
1990/91	Preceding year basis	6,000
		£19,500

Try to keep your taxable profits for the first year down to the minimum as this increases the benefits under the preceding year basis of assessment. This can be achieved by investing in your business equipment in the first year.

In some cases it may be worth starting up in business with your wife as an employee and bringing her into partnership after the first 12 months.

Paying into a private pension plan

If you do decide to draw your company pension and work part-time, don't forget that your part-time earnings will be non-pensionable earnings. Accordingly, you can obtain tax relief for personal pension premiums. These can offer an excellent return.

4.2.11   Example: personal pension premiums

A 71 year old man with part-time earnings of £5,000 could obtain tax relief for 'one-off' personal pension premiums of £1,000. The pension policy might provide for a lump sum and annuity to be taken from age 73. Assuming a marginal rate of tax of 40% the figures might work out like this:

Retirement annuity premium	£1,000
less tax relief	400
net cost	600
less tax free lump sum	260
	340

This exercise would currently result in an on-going pension of around £125 per annum—leaving the individual in a profit position after five years assuming he pays tax at 40 per cent on the pension.

Further reading

Allied Dunbar Pensions Guide by Tony Reardon.

5 Tackling tax

It would be foolish to try to ignore the effect of taxation. We all wish income tax had 'never happened' but the only sensible course of action is to calculate what is involved (ie 'compute' your tax liability) and then take whatever steps are available to reduce its impact. This chapter begins by setting out the way in which you can work out your income tax bill and describes the way in which capital gains tax operates. As part of this we deal with three matters:

- How is age allowance computed?
- How does top-slicing relief apply when you dispose of an investment bond?
- How does the CGT main residence exemption work?

5.1 Independent taxation

6 April 1990 was a landmark in UK taxation. From that date independent taxation took effect, under which each individual is responsible for his or her own tax affairs. Previously a married couple were taxed together, and the wife's income was usually added to the husband's who was then responsible for the tax. Married women now have to account to the Inland Revenue directly for their own tax. Because tax is now assessed individually, the Inland Revenue have introduced a new set of personal allowances.

5.1.1 Income tax

Each person will receive a single personal allowance, in addition to which there is a married couple's allowance, which is added to the husband's income but can be transferred to the wife if any part of it is unused. Higher allowances will be available for people over 65, provided their income falls within the stated limit.

As a consequence of these radical changes every married couple should review their financial position to take full advantage of the new reliefs. In particular it is highly beneficial for people with substantial incomes to ensure that, as far as possible, this is divided equally between them. Unnecessary amounts of tax will be paid if they do not do so. A simple example may help to explain this principle more clearly:

5.1.2   Example: independent taxation

Mr and Mrs A—Income to 6 April 1992. Mrs A has no income in her own right.

	Mr A	£	£
	Salary	30,000	
	Building society interest	5,000	
	Dividends	1,000	
		36,000	36,000
Less:	Single person's allowance	(3,295)	
	Married couple's allowance	(1,720)	
	Taxable	30,985	
	Tax at 25% on	23,700	(5,925)
	Tax at 40% on	7,285	(2,914)
	Net income		27,161

Mr A makes an outright gift of his building society account to Mrs A. The position would then be:–

	Mr A	£	£
	Salary	30,000	
	Dividends	1,000	
		31,000	31,000
Less:	Single person's allowance	(3,295)	
	Married couple's allowance	(1,720)	
	Taxable	25,985	
	Tax at 25% on	23,700	(5,925)
	Tax at 40% on	2,285	(914)
	Net income		24,161
	Mrs A		
	Building society interest	5,000	5,000
Less:	Single personal allowance	(3,295)	
	Tax at 25% on	1,705	(426)
			4,574

As a result of this change, their joint net income increases to £28,735 from £27,161.

Both spouses will be entitled to reliefs for losses, interest paid, pension contributions, etc against their own income.

Mortgage interest is treated somewhat differently. In this case an election can be made for the interest on a joint mortgage to be set against the highest income.

5.1.3 Capital Gains Tax

The principle of individual allowances has been extended to capital gains tax (CGT). Each partner of a marriage will be entitled to his or her own annual allowance (£5,500 for 1991/92). Gains arising on disposal of investments will be taxed as additional income at the rate applicable to the individual in the relevant year.

Using our previous example, if the assets producing dividends of £1,000 have appreciated sufficiently to give rise to a large gain then it might be sensible for Mr A to make an outright gift to Mrs A of all or part of the portfolio. That way any taxable gain arising on sale would be taxed at Mrs A's rate of 25% and not at Mr A's rate of 40%. Sufficient shares should be retained by Mr A to use his own annual CGT allowance, preferably those that produce the lowest income.

Transfers of assets between husband and wife are exempt from CGT, the recipient is deemed by the Inland Revenue to have acquired them at the cost of the transferor.

It is no longer possible to transfer gains and losses between husbands and wives.

5.1.4 Joint investments

It is common for married couples to hold their savings and investments in joint names. Where this is so, the Inland Revenue consider them to be held 50:50 and the income will be taxed accordingly. But where the actual ownership is different, for instance 75:25 ratio, a couple can make a declaration to that effect. This will enable them to be taxed on their fair share of the income.

Capital gains tax will be applied in much the same way as income tax. In the absence of a declaration the husband and wife will be regarded as owning half the asset each.

5.1.5   Summary

Independent taxation creates considerable opportunity for a married couple to reduce their overall tax burden through careful planning. Naturally it would be sensible to obtain professional guidance on this rather complicated subject.

5.2   Working out your tax bill

There are two main taxes which may affect you: income tax and capital gains tax.

5.2.1   Income tax

We have set out the stages in the income tax computation in the form of a flow chart. There should be sufficient information for most people but in cases of unusual complexity it may be necessary to refer to the *Allied Dunbar Tax Guide*.

Employees with share options should take professional advice to ensure that any income tax charge on the exercise of the options is kept as low as possible.

5.2.2   Table: working out your tax liability

			Tax paid
(1) *Compute earned income*			
National Insurance pension			
Occupational pension			
Retirement annuity			
Income from employment			
Freelance earnings	(i)	————	————
Deduct retirement annuity relief			
		————	————
	A	════	════

			Tax paid
(2) *Compute investment income*			
National Savings Bank interest	(ii)		
Income from abroad	(iii)		
Income from property	(iv)		
Dividends and taxed interest			
UK Bank and building society			
Interest			
		————	————
	B	════	════

(3) *Compute charges*			
Qualifying interest paid gross	(v)		
Interest paid subject to MIRAS	(vi)		
Amount paid under charitable			
deeds of covenant	(vii)		
		————	
	C	════	

(4) *Compute other deductions*
  Business expansion scheme
  relief   (viii)
  Allowable trading losses   (ix)

                                                                   D
                                                                   _____
                                                                   =======
                                                                                          Total

Total income (E)   A
                                                             B
                                                                   _____
Deduct   C & D
                                                             E
                                                                   _____
                                                                   =======

(5) *Compute personal allowances*
  Single person's allowance   (x)
  Married couple's allowance   (xi)

                                                             F
                                                                   _____
                                                                   =======

(6) *Tax liability*
Basically one deducts F from E and applies the following tables. However note position on items in E which quality only for higher rate relief, for example vi

0–23,700	25%
Over 23,700	40%

Notes:

(i)   This income will normally be assessable on the preceding year basis.
(ii)   There is an exemption for the first £70 interest credited each year on the NSB ordinary account.
(iii)   This income will normally be assessable on the preceding year basis.
(iv)   Does this include profits from furnished holiday accommodation? If so this counts as earned income.
(v)   This interest can be deducted from your taxable income for all tax purposes.
(vi)   Interest paid under MIRAS does not qualify for basic rate relief.
(vii) The deed must require payments for a period of at least four years. Basic rate is deducted at source so these payments are relevant only if you are subject to higher rate tax.
(viii) and (ix)   See *Allied Dunbar Tax Guide*.
(x)   Basic allowance is £3,295. Age Allowance can increase this to £4,020 if income does not exceed £13,500.
(xi)   Basic allowance is £1,720. Age Allowance can increase this to £2,355. Marginal Age Allowance can be claimed, the excess of taxable income over £13,500 results in a reduction of the allowance of £2 for every £3 excess income.

5.2.3   How is age allowance computed?

Age relief consists of an increase in your personal allowance of £725 (single) and £635 (married couple's). You are eligible for the relief if you or your wife has attained age 65 at any time during the tax year. The relief is, however, also dependent on your taxable income not exceeding a certain limit. If your income exceeds £13,500 the extra allowance is reduced by £1 for every £2 of excess income. If you or your spouse has attained age 75 then there is an increase of £675 in the married couple's allowance and £885 in the single person's allowance.

5.2.4   Example: age allowance

A has income of £13,620. The age addition to his personal allowance is therefore reduced by £60 ie ½ of the income over the £13,500 limit.

A useful example of how Age Allowance works can be found in the next chapter (see 6.4).

5.2.5   Top slicing relief on investment bonds

Insurance bonds can be tax efficient investments—but you need to use them in the right way. A higher rate income tax charge may arise on their eventual disposal and this charge applies to the overall profit.

5.2.6   Example: top slicing relief—investment bonds

A invests £10,000 in a bond on 1 January 1982. In March 1987 he cashes it in and receives £15,000. A's overall profit of £5,000 is not subject to the basic rate of 25% but is taxable at the higher rates if A is a higher rate tax payer because of his other income. Thus if A were subject to a top rate of tax of 40% there could be higher rate tax of 15% to pay on the profit of £5,000 (ie 40%–25%) so that tax of £750 would be payable.

5.2.7   Top slicing relief

Profits on the disposal of insurance bonds are normally an exceptional event and the tax legislation recognises this by giving top slicing relief. This is to enable gains to be 'spread' so that excessive tax is not payable because the exceptional income falls into just one year.

5.2.8 Example: top slicing relief—insurance bonds

Suppose that A's other income were such that only £3,000 of the £5,000 came within the 40% band and the £2,000 fell into the 25% band.

Before top slicing relief the tax payable would be:

£2,000 at 0%	0
£3,000 at 15%	450
	£450

When computing top slicing relief one divides the overall profit by the number of years that the policy has run, ie:

£5,000 divided by 5 = £1,000.

One then computes the extra tax found by adding that sum to A's other income, ie:

£1,000 at 0% = £0.

The tax on the £5,000 profit is £0, ie five (the number of policy years) x the tax on the notional amount of £1,000. The top slicing relief is therefore £450 (ie £450 less the actual tax liability of £0).

A similar tax charge can arise when amounts are taken out of a bond in excess of the tax free five per cent withdrawals. However, the computation is sometimes more complex and you should take professional advice.

5.3 Capital gains tax

Capital gains tax (CGT) is basically charged at 25 per cent or 40 per cent depending on the level of your other taxable income and is applied to gains realised from the disposal of chargeable assets. Losses of a capital nature may generally be deducted in arriving at the chargeable amount. For example, A has taxable income of £30,000 and is paying 40 per cent income tax on the top slice of his income. He realises total capital gains of £10,000 in a tax year. £4,500 suffers CGT at 40 per cent (the first £5,500 is exempt). There is normally no liability to CGT for transfers between husband and wife.

Your liability is worked out along the following lines:

5.3.1   Table: CGT liability

	Self	Wife
Gains on disposal of chargeable assets (see below)		
These are normally the net sale proceeds less cost		
Less indexation allowance	_____	_____
Less allowable losses on other disposals	_____	_____
Joint gains for year		
Less annual exemption		_____
Taxable at 25 per cent or 40 per cent		_____

Chargeable assets

A chargeable gain may arise on the disposal of any asset, other than an asset which is specifically exempt for CGT purposes. The following assets are regarded as exempt from CGT:

(1)   *Dwelling houses*—an individual is exempt from CGT insofar as he realises a gain on a property which has been his only or main residence or the only or main residence of a dependent relative.

(2)   *Chattels*—a tangible, movable asset is entirely exempt provided that the disposal proceeds do not exceed £6,000.

(3)   *Gilts*—Government securities and most corporate loan stocks are exempt from CGT. The position needs to be looked at more closely where company loan stocks were held prior to 14 March 1984.

(4)   *Debts*—no CGT normally arises on a disposal of a debt unless it is a 'debt on a security'. A debt on a security is normally a transferable debt such as a loan stock. In practice capital gains would not normally arise on the disposal of a debt and it is more probable that a capital loss would arise. Because debts are exempt assets for CGT purposes, no relief is normally available for losses which arise from the disposal of debts other than debts on a security.

(5)   *Foreign currency*—this is exempt provided that it was acquired for the owner's personal expenditure abroad. This includes the provision or maintenance of a residence abroad.

(6)   *Insurance policies*—the original owner of an insurance policy is not subject to CGT on the proceeds. You are also exempt if you were given the policy.

(7)   *Motor cars*—a vehicle constructed or adapted for the carriage of

passengers is exempt from CGT unless it is a vehicle of a type not commonly used as a private vehicle and unsuitable to be so used.

(8) *Savings certificates*—National Saving Certificates and other similar securities are not chargeable assets for CGT purposes.

Main residence exemption

In practice, most people are mainly concerned about the position on the disposal of their main residence and the flow chart in 13.4.1 should make the position clear.

Sale of a company or business

It is more difficult to avoid CGT on the sale of a business. By the very nature of things, a purchaser will wish there to be continuity of trading and will not just be acquiring assets which are used in a trade. Indeed, there will often be a significant element of goodwill in the price, and this definitely requires continuity. The problem is that a vendor will not be able to avoid CGT by deferring a sale until he has ceased to be UK resident.

Allowable deductions

We must now examine the deductions which may be claimed.

Value at 31 March 1982

If you owned the asset before 31 March 1982 and the value at that date was higher than the amount it cost you it may be possible to deduct the March 1982 value in arriving at your gain. The rule only came in for 1988/89 and does not apply to gains made before 6 April 1988. It is a straightforward matter to calculate the March 1982 value of quoted securities but where the asset is property or shares in a private company it will be necessary to negotiate a value with the Inland Revenue.

Indexation allowance

This is an allowance to compensate for the inflation which has occurred since 31 March 1982 and is computed by the formula

$$\frac{RD-RI}{RI} \text{ where:}$$

RD = the RPI for the month of disposal.
RI = the RPI for the month of acquisition or March 1982 if later.

5.3.2   Example: indexation allowance

C sells shares for £30,000 in March 1990
They cost £10,000 in 1969.
Their value at 31 March 1982 was £15,000.
The RPI for the month of disposal is 121.4.
The RPI for March 1982 was 79.4.
C can claim indexation allowance of:

$$\frac{121.4 - 79.4}{79.4} = 0.528 \times £15,000 = £7,920$$

and this is treated as a deduction in computing the chargeable gain.

Annual exemption

Another allowable item is the 'annual exemption'. This is currently £5,500. Note that the £5,500 is deducted from your capital gains and no unused part of the £5,500 can be carried forward.

The detailed CGT rules are very complicated and you may need to consult the *Allied Dunbar Tax Guide*. If you dispose of almost anything other than your main residence you may be well advised to consult a solicitor or accountant.

5.4   Tax planning

We can now focus on some tax planning aspects and address the following questions:

- How are termination payments taxed?
- When is the best time to retire if you are self-employed?
- How is CGT charged on the sale of a business?

5.4.1   Choosing the right date

It can make quite a lot of difference whether your employment is terminated at the beginning or end of a tax year. One situation where timing can be crucial is where a person receives a termination payment on early retirement. To understand this, it is necessary to go into some detail on the way in which compensation payments are taxed.

Compensation payments are known to the Inland Revenue as 'termination payments'. They are treated as income which arises at the date the employment terminates. It therefore makes no difference that the actual payment may be delayed until the next tax year; if A's employment ceased on 31 March 1991 his payment is assessed for 1990/91 even though it may be paid on 6 April 1991 or later during the tax year 1991/92.

A golden handshake is taxable in full as income if the director/employee is entitled to it under his contract of employment. In other cases there is an exemption for the first £30,000. This exemption applies whether the payment is expressed to be *ex gratia* or a compensation payment.

For the sake of completeness, it should also be mentioned that statutory redundancy payments are not themselves taxable, but they do consume part of the £30,000 exemption.

5.4.2 Example: compensation and redundancy

B receives compensation of £25,000 and statutory redundancy payments of £8,000. The redundancy payments are exempt, but mean that part of the compensation is taxable:

Compensation		£25,000
Exemption	£30,000	
Less	£8,000	£22,000
Taxable amount		£3,000

Where part of a termination payment becomes taxable it may be advantageous to apply the taxable element to augment pension. This is especially true where an employee is about to take early retirement and can enhance the tax free cash from the pension scheme.

Even when no more tax free cash can be provided, it is often the case that extra pension is better in the long run than taxable cash, particularly if tax on the termination payment is at the higher rates whereas pension suffers tax only at the basic rate.

5.4.3 Timing of retirement

It should now be obvious that the best time to terminate an employment is at the very start of a tax year if your marginal rate of tax will be lower after retirement. Any allowances not used to cover your other taxable income may be set against the part of your termination payment which exceeds £30,000.

There is also a planning point for the self-employed. Your retirement may give rise to a cessation for Schedule D purposes (see *Allied Dunbar Tax Guide*) and this means that the Inland Revenue may be able to increase your tax assessments for the two years preceding the year of your retirement. In some cases it may be worth deferring your retirement until shortly after 5 April, so as to limit the extent of the Inland Revenue's adjustments for past years.

The Revenue's powers arise from the fact that self-employed earnings are assessed on the preceding year basis. The Revenue are permitted to tax your actual earnings for the year of cessation and to adjust the assessments for the previous years if this results in an overall increase (the Revenue cannot just adjust one year in isolation).

5.4.4   Example: the self-employed

A is self-employed and has an accounting date of 30 June. His profits and tax assessments have been as follows:

		Assessed tax year
Year ended 30 June 1988	£12,000	1989/90
Year ended 30 June 1989	£15,000	1990/91
Year ended 30 June 1990	£20,000	1991/92
Year ended 30 June 1991	£25,000	1992/93

If A retires on 5 April 1992 and his last nine months' profits were £15,000 the Revenue would replace the 1991/92 assessment with the actual earnings for the year of £21,250 (ie 3 × 12 profits for the year to 30 June 1991 + the profits for the final nine months) and the two preceding years would be adjusted as follows:

1989/90:	3/12 × profits for year ended 30 June 1989	3,750
	9/12 × profits for year ended 30 June 1990	15,000
		18,750

1990/91:	3/12 × profits for year ended 30 June 1990	5,000
	9/12 × profits for year ended 30 June 1991	18,750
		23,750

Thus additional income would be assessed for 1989/90 of £6,750 and an adjustment of £8,750 would be made for 1990/91.

If A delayed his retirement until **6** April 1992, the Revenue could not adjust 1989/90 and the adjustments for the two following years would not be so great in total.

It is important to take professional advice on such a matter as the timing of a cessation. Special provisions apply where a person has been a member of a partnership.

5.4.5 Capital gains tax on the sale of your business/ private company

This is another area where the timing of your retirement may be very important. Even if you cannot avoid payments of CGT, it would obviously be more beneficial to dispose of your business/company on 6 April rather than 5 April. The additional delay in the payment of CGT for 12 months can be very valuable in these times of high interest rates.

It may, on the other hand, be possible to reduce the liability if the gain can be deferred until such time as you are entitled to the full CGT retirement relief.

This relief is available broadly speaking in the following circumstances:

(1)   the person realising the gain must be at least 55 or be forced to retire because of ill-health;
(2)   the person must have been engaged in the trade or have been a full-time working director of a family trading company;
(3)   the gain must arise on the sale of the business or shares in the family company or of an asset owned by the person but used rent free (or at a rent lower than the commercial rent) by the business or company.

The maximum relief is available only if the person has carried on business or been a full-time working director for the ten years preceding the disposal. Gains of up to £150,000 can be totally exempt and half of any gains between £150,000 and £600,000 can also be tax free.

Both husband and wife can qualify for the full relief if they meet the necessary conditions (for further details on this see *Allied Dunbar Tax Guide*).

The way in which the relief operates is complex and professional advice should be taken, but in principle you should time a disposal on retirement so as to ensure that full advantage is taken of the relief. All other things being equal if may pay to carry on another year rather than retire at (say) age 54 and pay substantial amounts of CGT.

5.4.6   Checklist for year of retirement

- Will it be beneficial to defer the date of your retirement because you will receive a termination payment?
- If you are self-employed, can you mitigate the tax consequences of a cessation of business on your retirement?
- Take advice on the sale of your private business or family company so as to minimise any capital gains tax.
- Can you pay further personal pension premiums?

5.4.7   Leaflets available from any HM Inspector of Taxes Office

Subject	*Reference Number*
Residents and Non-Residents—	
Liability to tax in the United Kingdom	IR20
Tax and your Business—Starting in business	IR28
Income Tax, Capital Gains Tax and Inheritance	
Tax—What happens when someone dies	IR45
Employed or Self Employed?	IR56/N139
Thinking of working for yourself?	IR57
Personal Pensions. A new pensions choice —a	
guide for tax	IR87
Independent Taxation—A Guide for Married	
Couples	IR80
Independent Taxation—A Guide for Pensioners	IR81
Independent Taxation—A Guide for Husbands on	
a Low Income	IR82
Independent Taxation—A Guide to Allowances	
and Reliefs	IR90
Independent Taxation—A Guide for Widows and	
Widowers	IR91
Private Medical Insurance	IR103
Can you stop paying tax on your bank and	
building society interest?	IR110
Capital Gains Tax—Owner-occupied houses	CGT4
Capital Gains Tax—Retirement on Disposal of a	
business	CGT6
Capital Gains Tax and Small Businesses	CGT11
Capital Gains Tax—An Introduction	CGT14
Capital Gains Tax—A Guide For Married Couples	CGT15

Further reading

Allied Dunbar Capital Taxes and Estate Planning Guide by Walter Sinclair and P D Silke.
Allied Dunbar Tax Guide by Walter Sinclair.

6 Investment and savings

Even if you have the maximum pension, there will still be some reduction in your income at the very time that you have more opportunity to enjoy the things that money can buy. Furthermore, the gap between your pension and your expenditure is likely to grow because of inflation. This is where your savings come in: invested judiciously they will produce the extra income that you need and bridge the gap between your expenditure and pension to maintain your income as you grow older.

6.1 Adopting the right strategy

Your investment policy, or 'strategy' should be based on your personal circumstances. The right strategy for you may not be appropriate for someone else. Before we go into this, answer the following questions:

- What spendable income do you need *now*?
- What provision do you think you should make against inflation?
- How would your spouse stand for income if you were to die in five, or ten, or fifteen years' time?
- What rate of tax applies to your investment income?
- Is this likely to change significantly in the future?
- How much of your capital do you need to keep readily available?
- Can you set aside *some* of your capital and invest this for the medium term so as to secure a better return?
- Should you pay off the mortgage?

To some extent you need to strike a balance between various considerations. You certainly do need to have ready access to some of your capital in case of an emergency but it is probably wrong for you to invest all your capital in (say) a building society or high interest bank account. It is wrong since:

- it may be 'inefficient' from a tax point of view in that you may be paying more tax than you need
- the value of your capital will not increase
- your real income will at best be static and may actually fall—when you take account of inflation.

Older people tend to be conservative investors—and rightly so, but there is really no such thing as a 'riskless' investment. A building society or bank account seems to be risk-free since you can always withdraw £100 for every £100 that you put in. However, it carries a hidden risk that the capital value may be eroded and the interest paid out may fall if interest rates go down in the future. So an apparently risk-free investment may actually leave you exposed twice over—the level of your interest income may go down at a time when you need more income to take care of inflation.

By contrast, asset-backed investments such as insurance bonds and unit trusts are certainly not risk-free investments, the value of your units may go down as well as up—especially in the short term. But in some respects these broadly based, asset-backed investments may seem a better bet in the long run, for both the income and capital growth investor. The table below shows what has happened over the past ten years on a building society account and a UK unit trust. Not only has the unit trust produced more income, it has also increased the value of the capital.

6.1.1. Table: Income growth. Unit trusts vs building societies *(Source—Unit Trust Association)*

Net Income per Annum £

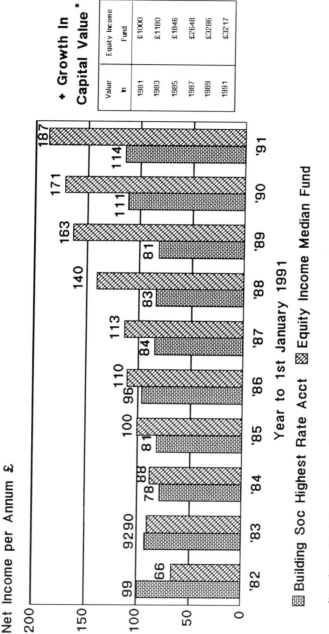

+ Growth In Capital Value *

Value In	Equity Income Fund
1981	£1000
1983	£1180
1985	£1846
1987	£2648
1989	£3286
1991	£3217

Year to 1st January 1991

Building Soc Highest Rate Acct   Equity Income Median Fund

Above figures relate to the annual income paid by the median performing UK Equity Income Fund and a Building Society Highest Rate Account.

* The Building Society highest rate account does not provide any capital growth on the original £1,000 invested.

The point we are making is *not* that you should necessarily invest most of your money in shares or unit trusts. This may or may not be appropriate according to your personal circumstances, your views on the economy etc. What we are saying is that you should ask yourself who was really the more cautious investor—the person who kept all his money in a building society or a person who accepted a lower level of income on some of his capital because he expected the income to rise? By applying the following ground rules you will avoid most of the pitfalls:

(1)   There must be ready access to some capital.
(2)   Any portfolio that is established with the primary objective of producing spendable income should be arranged in such a way as to produce a regular cash flow. Few retired people will wish to receive their income on an annual or half yearly basis. Income should be as regular as is practicable, and the choice of investments should be made with this requirement in mind.
(3)   Equity and property based investments should also play some part.
(4)   Undue risk should be avoided as far as possible—including the possibility of a serious reduction in interest rates.
(5)   Such investments need to be *managed* and unit-linked insurance funds and unit trusts are especially appropriate for the smaller investor.
(6)   Consistently good performance is the most important thing to look for when choosing a unit trust or insurance group.
(7)   Tax needs to be borne in mind. Insurance bonds may be an especially attractive way for a higher rate tax payer to invest. Also bear in mind investments which provide a tax free return such as National Savings Certificates, PEPs and TESSAs.
(8)   Bear in mind the fact that tax free spendable 'income' can often be produced by taking capital gains, eg on shares or unit trusts, within the annual CGT exemption. Looked at in simplistic terms £55,000 growing at 10 per cent per annum could produce £5,500 net 'income' from capital gains whereas a 40 per cent taxpayer would need to have £91,667 on deposit at 10 per cent in order to have £5,500 spendable income after tax.
(9)   Don't make the mistake of investing for the highest immediate income. Take a long term view and look into assets that will produce a growing income.

Much of this is self-evident, but it is easy to overlook.

6.1.2 Putting these principles into practice

It's impossible to say how much should go into any particular type of investment, as each portfolio will be arranged to suit individual circumstances. However, most people will not want to lock all their money up immediately in long-term investments, but rather will take the view that part should be kept for short-term use, some may be needed after five years, and the balance can be salted away for long-term investment. By adopting this approach, certain categories of investment will automatically select themselves.

Within three years

This is the cash you just feel you might need in the next couple of years. Some will need to be available immediately—the remainder can be on longer-term deposit to obtain a higher return.

How much money do you feel should be immediately accessible? £500? £1,000? Whatever amount you feel is right should go into your building society, or into one of the interest bearing current accounts, which allows withdrawals without notice.

How much more do you feel comfortable about being available at, say three months' notice? Perhaps you would feel easier in your mind if you were able to fund holidays and contingencies (eg a major repair to the car) over the next two or three years. That's the amount that should go into a building society offering the best rates you can find, which will normally entail having to give notice.

What this will provide is a cushion against unexpected emergencies, and also against adverse investment conditions elsewhere. It will also enable you to plan your other investments without worrying about whether you will have the money. On the other side of the coin, a float will provide the means to take an unexpected investment opportunity. You will also get a high level of income.

Three to five years

This is the money you will feel happier about if you know it's going to be back in your hands within five years. As this is still a relatively short period you should put the money required during this period into gilts and National Savings.

Gilts: Even though, at the time of writing, real interest rates are historically high, there is the possibility that over the medium term these will fall. High coupon gilts offer a flexible means of guaranteeing a fixed income for a pre-determined period. If interest rates do fall, it may be possible to sell the stock and make a tax free capital gain.

For those who do not need income, there is a choice of gilts that will produce guaranteed capital growth. These are the low coupon stocks, which stand at a price below the redemption value; or the index-linked stocks where the value is increased in line with inflation. Both are useful vehicles for providing a safe and risk free home for short-term capital.

National Savings Certificates: The tax exempt nature of this investment, and the competitive returns they offer, make them particularly attractive to the higher rate taxpayer. Like gilts, they can be purchased on the basis of a fixed return, or an index-linked basis. National Savings Certificates can also be used to provide the investor with capital growth or income (see 7.5.4).

More than five years

This is where equities, and equity-based investments such as unit trusts and investment bonds come into the reckoning (indeed they are longer-term investments and you shouldn't be looking at them as shorter-term investments). Invest for income if that's what you need, but look forward to capital growth over the long term as well.

It is perfectly possible to construct a portfolio of unit trusts specifically designed to provide you with an income. Unit trusts usually make income payments every six months, six unit trusts with phased payment dates packaged together can therefore provide a monthly income. These 'monthly income plans' are marketed by the major companies and are increasingly used to supplement income in retirement. The capital value of the investment will fluctuate (one only has to look back to 1974 and October 1987) but the overall level income from a widely spread portfolio of shares (which is what a unit trust is) has remained remarkably steady over the years.

Used as a vehicle to provide a spendable 'income' and capital growth, the managed bond can also play a useful and rewarding role. This is especially true where the investor is a higher rate taxpayer at the time the bond is established, but his rate of tax is reduced to the basic rate when the bond is encashed.

A judicious combination of these investments should fulfil all the criteria laid down in our investment policy. As a result, your investment returns should be good and much of the concern that is associated with investment should be eliminated. You will, of course, need to review the position regularly, to ensure that you are obtaining the best possible terms.

6.2 Inflation

Until recently, inflation faced investors with an unwelcome choice. If they selected very secure investments to safeguard their capital, they faced the certainty that it would be gradually eroded as the purchasing power of money declined. If, on the other hand, they chose less secure investments whose value was likely to increase to compensate for inflation, they ran the risk of suffering a loss. The traditional inflation hedges of shares and property are well known for the fact that their value can go down as well as up.

The chief sufferers from this were the small investors who were dependent upon their savings. As a result, it was to these people that the remedy of index linking was first made available. Unfortunately, the original index linked investments, granny bonds, were not particularly attractive. Despite this, large sums of money were put into them as their availability was widened. More recently, a much more attractive inflation protected investment has been made available in the form of index linked gilts. Initially, however, they could only be bought by pension funds. After a year the restriction was removed, and everyone is now free to buy index linked government stock. The result has been to give everyone the opportunity of complete protection against inflation. The potential of this is clearly very great, but so far few private investors have taken advantage of the opportunity.

Although inflation has receded as a threat, it certainly has not disappeared, and could easily re-emerge as the dominant investment consideration. Between 1976 and 1982, prices doubled. This meant that if your investment did not grow by more than 100 per cent, you actually got poorer. As in *Alice Through The Looking Glass*, it took all the running you could do to stay in the same place. If you want to get somewhere else, you must run twice as fast as that.

If prices are stable, cash represents a safe investment. In an inflationary world, this is not so. A pound tomorrow will be worth less than a pound today. Even a rate of five per cent can have a serious effect: inflation at five per cent for ten years means that unless your capital has grown in value by 63 per cent you are actually poorer. In the past, of course, things have been much worse.

During the ten years to 1982 prices rose 200 per cent, and at the end of the period things cost three and a half times as much as they did in

1970. In other words, in 1982 you needed one pound to buy what could be purchased for 5s 11d in 1970. Some things have gone up even more. A London evening paper in 1970 cost 6d (2½p), while its successor in 1986 cost 20p—an increase of 700 per cent over 16 years. Although this appears an enormous increase, it actually represents an average rate of inflation of only 14 per cent pa. It takes very few years of double digit inflation to increase prices several hundred per cent.

There is no complete solution to the problem of inflation where the rate of price increases outstrips the return you can obtain on your investments. It is therefore important to ensure that, to as great a degree as possible, your investments are arranged in such a way as to produce the best return while retaining sufficient flexibility in order that they can be adapted to changing investment and inflationary conditions.

6.3   Paying off the mortgage

It is by no means uncommon for a person to reach retirement and find that there is still a mortgage outstanding on the main residence. While this in many cases may not be a particularly substantial amount, it nevertheless is worth considering whether or not to pay it off.

6.3.1   Flexibility

Most people if they had much choice would rather be without the burden of a mortgage and consequently it is quite natural that when the opportunity arises they repay the amount in full, usually with a sigh of relief. Such an opportunity normally occurs at retirement, when endowment policies mature and, more commonly, a lump sum from a pension scheme is received. But is it wise to repay the mortgage? There are a number of factors to consider. Firstly, there is the question of flexibility. Once capital is used up for this purpose it cannot normally be recalled if it is ever needed again. For example, a sizeable sum may be required to finance an expensive purchase such as a new car or holiday home. By not repaying the building society and keeping the cash in the bank you retain flexibility. It can of course be argued that after repaying the loan you can always remortgage your home if money is needed urgently, but this can be a troublesome and expensive exercise which you could well do without.

6.3.2   Tax relief

Tax relief could be an important consideration. Even if you have no need to hold on to the cash it might be worthwhile to maintain the mortgage so that you continue to benefit from the tax relief. What needs to be clarified is whether tax relief is actually enjoyed in your particular case.

Under many of the older style repayment mortgages relief was given in the early years of the loan and this ran off as the years passed. Your tax office can tell you what mortgage interest relief is available to you. By contrast mortgages arranged on the endowment method will almost certainly enjoy tax relief right up to the time the mortgage is repaid by the life policy.

6.3.3 Investing to pay the mortgage

It must be conceded, however, that while some may find the benefits of flexibility and tax relief cogent arguments for retaining a mortgage, others will conclude that the burden of meeting the monthly repayments is sufficient reason to extinguish the debt. In the latter case a solution may be found in setting aside capital equivalent to the mortgage in an appropriate investment and using the income to meet the repayments. For example, A has a mortgage of £10,000 under which net repayments amount to £90 per month. Instead of paying off the mortgage £10,000 is invested in a building society account paying interest at seven per cent net. On a monthly income plan this would generate £58, thus leaving only £32 to be found from income. This is not a complete answer to the problem of meeting repayments but it considerably mitigates the burden. Remember, if an investment can produce a net return of 11 per cent a year then the whole of the repayments can be met and the capital retained at the same time.

6.3.4 Endowment loans

If an endowment mortgage is repaid early, what should happen to the endowment policy? Certainly it could be surrendered and the proceeds may well be sufficient to pay off the loan. But if the policy has only a few years left to run the surrender value may not be as attractive as the sum payable if the contract is held to maturity. In many cases this situation results in the policy being retained when the mortgage is repaid, with the effect that only part of the monthly commitments is eliminated.

The final decision will, as with many things, depend on personal financial circumstances and preferences.

6.3.5 Lifetime loans

A concept that has gained ground recently is that of the lifetime loan. Usually loans, such as a building society mortgage are repaid after a specified number of years. The lifetime loan changes that tradition by extending the term of the borrowing to repayment at the death of the borrower or on the sale of the property, whichever comes first.

This can be of interest to those retiring who find that they have a loan to be repaid, for example from the proceeds of an endowment or pension policy. By converting the mortgage on to a lifetime basis, the cash from the policy can be retained. Of course this means that the interest payments must go on beyond retirement, but there is compensating income from the capital when it is invested. Thus the benefit of flexibility is retained.

6.3.6   Investor protection

The passing of the Financial Services Act 1986 ushered in a formidable body of legislation designed to protect investors' interests and ensure that they received professional advice. The scope of the Act is extremely wide and covers almost all sectors of the financial market.

We are not concerned here with every aspect of the Financial Services Act but rather focus on how the legislation benefits the private investor. The main thrust of the Act has been to enforce more stringent controls over companies that operate in the financial services industry. For example, it makes certain that they have adequate resources to run their businesses, that staff are sufficiently well trained and competent, and clients' money is kept entirely separate from that of the company's other income and capital.

6.3.7   How are advisers controlled?

All these regulations must of course be enforced, and for this purpose the Securities and Investment Board (SIB) has been established. Its job is to enforce the Financial Services Act and it has jurisdiction over the financial giants, such as insurance and unit trust groups, as well as the small adviser. The SIB does not in every case exercise direct control over the myriad financial concerns but delegates much of its policing function to various governing bodies called Self Regulatory Organisations (SROs). It is the SROs' duty to ensure that their members comply with the complex Conduct of Business Rules laid down under their respective rulebooks.

6.3.8   Choice of adviser

Financial advice is available from a number of different sources. Traditionally it has perhaps come more from the bank manager, accountant, solicitor or stockbroker. In recent years the field has widened to include insurance companies and insurance brokers setting up specialist departments to provide investment and financial services. All are controlled by their respective SRO. In the case of the accountant and the solicitor it is the Recognised Professional Body (RPB) that acts as the SRO. Insurance companies are controlled by LAUTRO whereas most independent financial advisers are members of FIMBRA. Each SRO has its own set of rules and its members have to operate within them—failure to do could lead to a loss of authorisation and the business may well have to close.

6.3.9   Maintaining standards

As part of the process of ensuring that the public receives a sufficiently high standard of advice, companies must register individual employees and agents with their SRO. They have the power to refuse to register individuals if they are not considered to be 'fit and proper'. It is only those considered 'fit and proper' who will be empowered to sell financial products or offer investment advice. It is a criminal offence to conduct an investment business or give financial advice without the necessary authorisation or exemption and those who do so risk a term of imprisonment.

6.3.10   Terms of business

Depending on the type of advice or the service you require, you should normally agree in advance with your adviser the basis on which you transact business. Accordingly, you should receive a Terms of Business letter or a Client Agreement setting out exactly the terms and conditions that will govern all transactions.

6.3.11   Best advice

A foundation stone of the Financial Services Act is the requirement for advisers to give 'best advice'. This obligation in essence means that where a financial product is recommended it must be the one that suits the client's individual needs.

To ensure that 'best advice' is given it is mandatory for an adviser to 'know the client'. Clearly, unless your individual circumstances are fully considered it will be impossible to take account of all the relevant factors before formulating a recommendation. Consequently a lengthy client questionnaire may be needed for this purpose and records must be kept showing how a decision was arrived at. These documents must be available for inspection for up to seven years.

6.3.12   Polarisation

The concept of polarisation has also been introduced in relation to the sale of life assurance and unit trust products. This seeks to differentiate between independent and non-independent sources of advice. Into the former category will fall the independent financial advisory firms (brokers), accountants, solicitors, etc. These have access to all financial products and are not tied to any one particular company. Non-independents are practitioners who are bound to one company or financial services group. The most obvious example here is the company representative whose job it is to promote his particular firm's products. Estate agents, banks and building societies may also fit into this category.

The object of polarisation is to enable investors to recognise whether they are dealing with independent advisers or a company representative or tied agent. Care must nevertheless be exercised to ensure that an adviser has the knowledge and resources available to provide a first class service. An adviser must also be able to draw on the expertise of specialists in order to provide comprehensive and detailed solutions to complex problems. The independent firms must therefore be large enough to retain a range of experts who can provide advice on matters such as tax and legal matters. A company representative will normally have access to a technical department that is competent to deal with a wide range of subjects.

6.4   Tax and your investments

Investments are taxed in different ways, depending upon their nature. The higher your tax rate, the more important this is. An investment which is appropriate for a person who pays tax at the higher rates may be unattractive to someone who pays no tax.

There is simple rule for dealing with tax—always work out what the net return will be for you after tax. This is all that matters. Advertisements often like to quote gross yields. This is understandable, since the figures are much larger. Unfortunately, most of us will only receive our income after paying tax on it.

The taxation of capital gains has been brought more into line with the tax on income. Anyone who makes a capital gain on their investment has the gain added to their taxable income. They will then be taxed at the appropriate rate applicable to income at that level but only after taking into account the following allowance:

(1) *The annual allowance.* The first £5,500 of your net gains for 1991/ 92 are exempt from tax.

(2) Most capital losses which you realise can be deducted in arriving at your chargeable capital gains.

(3) *Indexation.* A deduction can be made from the gain to take account of the effects of inflation; also any loss that you make can be increased.

(4) Certain assets that produce capital gains are exempt from CGT, ie Government Stock and National Savings Certificates.

Clearly, the taxation of capital gains is much more favourable than the profits or income derived from interest bearing investments. It is, therefore, sensible when planning your investments to take account of the differences in taxation so as to ensure that you suffer the lowest overall rate of tax. However, investment return is the most important requirement, you should never let the 'tax tail wag the investment dog'.

It is not just those who are subject to higher rate tax who need to consider this aspect. You may, for example, be caught by the age allowance 'trap'.

As we have seen you may be entitled to an increased personal allowance once you (or your wife) has attained the age of 65. The single person's allowance is increased to £4,020 and the married couple's allowance is increased to £2,355. However, the increased allowance is available only if your total taxable income is below £13,500. If it goes over that limit you lose £1 of the extra allowance for every £2 of extra income. So you pay twice: 25 per cent tax on the excess income plus 25 per cent on the amount of the allowance lost— in practice it is the same as paying tax at 37.5 per cent on the top 'slice' of your income.

What can be done about this? Consider investing some capital in insurance bonds. You may actually be able to increase your net spendable income.

6.4.1 Example: insurance bonds

Let us take a case where a married man has income of £16,220 from invested capital and assume that the capital is earning income at 6 per cent per annum. If the person were to invest £45,333 in an insurance bond he might reduce his taxable income to below £13,500 but increase his spendable income by taking the tax free 5 per cent withdrawals each year (until 100 per cent of the original has been withdrawn).

	'Before' £	'After' £
Income at 6% on capital invested	16,220	13,500
Less married age allowance	5,015	6,375
Taxable income	11,205	7,125
Tax thereon at 25%	2,801	1,781
Add 5% withdrawal from insurance bond	NIL	2,266
Spendable income	13,419	13,985

Bond are also a very attractive way for higher rate tax payers to invest. If you would otherwise pay at 40 per cent the value of the five per cent withdrawals is equivalent to taxable income of 8.3 per cent.

7 Investment options—interest-linked

These are investments where the return is governed by interest rates. This covers a broad range of investments. In some cases the capital value is fixed but the interest may fluctuate; in other cases, the reverse applies. In yet other cases the return varies according to inflation. However, whilst there is a variety, the basic feature of these investments is that they are not 'risk' investments. We start by looking at fixed capital investments.

Whatever your circumstances, you need to keep at least a part of your assets in some form of fixed capital investment, even if it is only a comparatively small reserve for the proverbial rainy day. There is a great variety of this type of investment, but these types can be narrowed down to a few which offer the best solutions for the great majority of investors, and that are applicable to most investors, and we outline those that are most commonly used by the public as a home for their savings.

7.1 Building societies

The most basic building society investment is the ordinary share. The great attraction of this is that you can lay your hands on your money whenever you want it. In addition, it pays a competitive rate of interest. However, though building society ordinary shares are popular, they are not necessarily the best place for retired people to keep a significant part of their capital. If you can put in the money so that it is subject to 90 days' notice of withdrawal, you may earn as much as three per cent per annum extra interest over the ordinary share rate. In practice you are highly unlikely to need a large sum of money without any warning. Even if you do, the penalties are relatively modest, the loss of 90 days' interest may be outweighed by the extra interest that you have earned in the past few years. As a result, the advantage of immediate accessibility is of little use to retired people. They can do much better by tying their money up for a little longer.

Until recently, the terms offered by building societies were all much the same, although a few of the smaller ones offered slightly higher rates. Today, the situation has become much more competitive and it certainly makes sense to look around before deciding where to place your money. Once you have chosen a society you should regularly review the market in order to make sure that you cannot do better elsewhere. A number of newspapers and financial magazines publish surveys of building society investments from time to time. It is still generally true that the best terms are available from some of the smaller specialist societies. They are able to offer them because they tend to provide higher priced mortgages.

Certain investors shy away from putting money with a small society. It is doubtful whether this is a sensible reaction if it is a member of the Building Societies Association. In the past, when one of the members has got into trouble, the others have rallied round and protected the investors from loss.

7.2   Tax exempt special savings accounts (TESSAs)

Lump sum investors who are looking for capital growth or spendable income should take a close look at a TESSA. Under the regulations laid down by the Inland Revenue, the interest on the account can be accumulated or drawn as income. Where income is taken the tax credit is added to the account and, provided the capital is untouched, forms the bonus at the end of the five year term. As a tax efficient and secure investment a TESSA is a clear winner.

7.3   Government stock

Government stocks, 'gilts', are also a very attractive form of interest bearing investments but they are also one of the least used by the private investor. Perhaps this is because they can seem complicated compared to other interest bearing investments. There are a large number of different issues of Government stock each with its own unique characteristics. Most of them are due to be redeemed either on a fixed date or within a certain period of time. The attraction for the Government of having a certain amount of latitude over the timing is that it can choose to redeem the stock when conditions are favourable. If it is tied to a fixed date, the money must be repaid regardless of the circumstances. The stock is normally denominated in units of £100 (known as the 'nominal' or 'par' value) and this is the amount which will be repaid on redemption.

Every stock pays interest and this is normally done every six months. The rate of interest varies greatly from one issue to another. Some stock is known as having a 'high coupon', and pays a high rate of interest such as 10, 11 or 12 per cent whereas other issues are known as 'low coupon' stocks and these may pay out three, four or five per cent.

As well as differences in the interest rate, the stocks have different redemption dates. Some are due to be repaid within a matter of months whereas others will not be until well into the next century. Stocks with less than five years to redemption are generally known as 'shorts' and those with between five and 15 years are known as 'medium'. Over 15 years defines a 'long'. There are even a few issues of 'undated' stock which may never be redeemed.

Government stocks are traded on the Stock Exchange and their value is liable to fluctuate. Clearly, the value of any one stock is unlikely to be far from the par value of £100 when it is close to its redemption date. On the other hand, if redemption is many years in the future the value of the stock can fluctuate considerably as interest rates move up and down.

When other interest rates are high the price of Government stocks will be low in value so as to produce a matching compatible return. Conversely, as rates fall, the stock value will rise. The greatest fluctuations are seen in undated stock and those with redemption dates which are far in the future. For this reason, those who wish to minimise the risks they are running are well advised to restrict their investments to the short dated issues which are conventionally taken to be those whose redemption is no more than five years ahead.

The prices of gilt edged stock are shown in the leading newspapers and beside them will be shown different figures indicating the return which is available to an investor. These may differ from the nominal interest which the stock pays. The reason for this is that the price is likely to be considerably removed from the par value of £100. It may be either higher or lower. If it is below par value when it is bought and held right up to redemption the holder can expect to receive a capital gain in addition to the income that will be paid on the stock.

7.3.1 Index-linked Government stock

Public interest was limited when index-linked gilts were originally introduced. One reason for this was that the private investor was not able to buy them. This was quickly changed but they were less attractive since inflation was falling. There are now no less than 12 different index-linked government stocks with redemption dates ranging from 1992 to 2024.

The index-linked government stock or 'gilts' work in exactly the same way as conventional gilts except that the nominal value and the interest payments are adjusted to take account of the fall in the value of money. The adjustment effectively increases their value by the rise in the Retail Price Index. The value of this naturally depends much upon the future rate of inflation. If it is low then the value of the inflation protection is small. If the economy does less well and inflation is high, it will be correspondingly enhanced.

Although the nominal value and the interest are index-linked this does not mean that the security will retain the same real value all the time. It is traded on the Stock Exchange and its price will vary according to demand, just as that of any other government stock does. However, if you buy stock and hold it to redemption you know exactly what return you will get in terms of real purchasing power.

If you sell it in the interim, you may do either better or worse, depending upon how the market has moved in the meantime. During the few years this stock has been in existence, it has been much less affected by changes in interest rates than are conventional gilts. At the present price levels all the index-linked stocks promise a running yield (annual income) of around 2.75–3.75 per cent on top of any index linking. Allowing for the addition of capital gain to redemption, real returns are around four per cent.

It is difficult to compare an index-linked investment with a conventional one. It all depends on what the rate of inflation will be in the future, and this cannot be forecast accurately. If you are interested in putting some of your money into this sort of investment you may need to get expert advice.

7.4   Off-shore 'roll-up funds'

We have previously mentioned how these operate (see 1.7.8) and the way in which the tax bill is deferred until the investor realises his investment. These funds are for all practical purposes the equivalent of having money on deposit in the Isle of Man and the Channel Islands and the tax treatment can make them most attractive. An investor could, for example, use an investment in such a fund to take an annual 'income', much of which could be tax free.

7.4.1 Example: Off-shore 'roll-up funds'

An investor has £100,000 in a sterling fund which achieves growth of 12 per cent per annum. If £12,000 is drawn off each year the following amounts will be subject to income tax:

Year 1	1285	Year 6	5921
Year 2	2434	Year 7	6572
Year 3	3459	Year 8	7154
Year 4	4374	Year 9	7673
Year 5	5191	Year 10	8136

This effect arises because the amount that is charged is the gain computed according to CGT rules. Thus the gain in Year 1 is computed as follows:

	£
Sale Proceeds	12,000
Cost $12,000 \times \dfrac{100,000}{100,000 + 12,000}$	10,715
Gain	1,285

7.5 National Savings

In recent years the Government has placed a good deal of emphasis on keeping the rates of interest offered on the various National Savings investments competitive with their market rivals. It is now possible to obtain a worthwhile return and enjoy complete security of capital by investing in this way. In addition, National Savings pay interest without deduction of tax at source.

7.5.1 National Savings Income Bonds

Interest is paid on a monthly basis without deduction of tax. The interest rate is variable and subject to notice of change. You may cash part of your holding in multiples of £1,000, but you must keep a minimum of £2,000 invested. There are stringent penalties if you wish to redeem all or part of your capital at short notice which could mean forfeiting some or all of the interest.

7.5.2 National Savings Indexed Income Bond

Based on a term of ten years, the bond is designed to pay a high level of income which rises in line with inflation. The starting rate is eight per cent per annum before tax and the income is paid out monthly. At the end of each year the sum is increased sufficiently to offset the rate of inflation over the previous years. The drawback is that while the income goes up, the capital value remains static so that no protection from inflation is offered in respect of the sum invested. Redemption terms are the same as those under the Income Bond.

7.5.3   National Savings Deposit Bond

This bond is designed to attract those who like an interest bearing investment which capitalises the interest rather than paying it as income. As with the Income Bond, interest is credited gross. Repayment is at three months' notice, but there is an interest penalty if the investment is redeemed within one year of purchase.

7.5.4   National Savings Certificates (Fixed interest variety)

No interest is paid, but after a stated period, usually five years, the certificates can be redeemed at a higher value than the issue price. Certificates may be encashed with an increased value after one year, but the rate of interest is progressive and the full return can only be obtained by holding the certificates for the full term. The capital gain is free of all tax.

These certificates can also be used to produce an income. In effect this can be achieved by cashing a specified number of certificates each year to cream off the appreciation and at the end of the period the remaining certificates will repay the original investment. As the gain is tax free this can be an extremely tax efficient means of providing spendable income for the higher rate taxpayer.

7.5.5   Example: National Savings Certificates (Fixed interest)

32nd Issue yielding 8.75% if held for five years:

Investment of £5,000.00 secures 200 certificates.

End of year	Certificates cashed	Income	% Interest
1	16	426.08	8.52
2	15	429.45	8.58
3	14	435.54	8.71
4	12	410.28	8.20
5	11	418.33	8.36

Remaining 132 certificates repay £5,019.96.

This exercise can be undertaken with most issues, and the number of certificates encashed is approximately the same in each case.

7.5.6 Index-Linked National Savings Certificates

Provided the certificates are held for more than a year the redemption value is equal to the original purchase price, increased in proportion to the increase in the Retail Prices Index which has occurred between the month of the purchase and the month of redemption. In addition to this, holders can also receive a supplementary payment, but to obtain the maximum yield certificates must be held for the full five years. Once again, the capital gain is free of all taxes and the certificates guarantee to provide a return which beats inflation.

7.6 Insurance company schemes

Insurance companies have had income producing investments for many years. Where a regular level of income is required, an insurance company scheme could be useful. Unfortunately, they are a little complicated, but nevertheless they have proved popular for those who are prepared to tie up part of their capital for five to ten years.

These schemes comprise two separate parts:

(1)   Temporary annuity
(3)   Endowment assurance policy.

Most of your capital investment is applied to purchase a temporary annuity providing a level income. The annuity payments may be made yearly (starting one year from the date you start your plan) or monthly (commencing one month after the starting date), and will be made directly to your bank account.

The balance of your capital investment is the first premium on the endowment assurance policy. The second and subsequent premiums are met from the net annuity payments and will normally be paid by direct debiting mandate from your bank account.

The combination of annuity and endowment will provide:

Income Any payments from the annuity not used to fund the regular premiums under the bond are available as net income.

Capital The proceeds of the endowment assurance policy at the end of the period should repay the capital.

There is no guarantee that the amount repaid by the insurance company at the end of the term years will equal the original investment. This is dependent on investment returns during the life of the policy.

It is of course important to understand that in order to obtain the full benefit from this type of plan it has to be maintained for the full term.

7.7 Guaranteed income bonds

As the name indicates, these 'bonds' guarantee a rate of income for a specific period of time. They are usually deferred annuities, or single premium endowment policies maturing every year to provide income with a policy expiring at the end of the period to repay the capital.

The tax treatment is somewhat complex, but as with most other life insurance schemes there is no liability to a basic rate tax payer. A higher rate tax payer may suffer a tax charge on the gain at the difference between the higher rate less the basic rate.

Guaranteed income bonds are an excellent means of locking into prevailing interest rates. As such they should form a part of every portfolio.

7.8 Annuities

The traditional investment for a retired person used to be a purchased life annuity. In its usual form, you pay a lump sum to an insurance company, which then promises to pay you an income for however long you live.

What you get from an annuity depends on the following factors:

- interest rates generally available at the time you purchase the annuity,
- your age at the time you start the annuity,
- your sex.

If you are a man of, say, 65 when you buy your annuity you have a life expectancy of about 15 years. The insurance company constructs the annuity to repay the capital to you over those 15 years and pay interest on the outstanding capital. The repayments (which therefore consist of partly repaid capital and interest) are calculated so that they are equal for the rest of your life, even if you live longer than 15 more years.

As a result, for any given purchase price, an annuity is higher for older people (and it will obviously be higher if interest rates at the time are high). On the other hand annuities for women are lower because all the available evidence shows that women live longer than men.

The interest 'element' is taxed at source but the tax can be reclaimed if you are a non taxpayer.

There is a wide variety of annuities and you can arrange to have the income paid every month, quarter, half year or year. You can also buy an annuity which will pay out a certain minimum amount, regardless of whether you survive. One arrangement which is particularly popular is the so called capital protected annuity. In this, the insurance company guarantees to return the purchase price of the annuity, either in a series of payments while you are alive, or by making up the difference by a lump sum when you die. A pension is a form of annuity and this is usually arranged on the basis of monthly payments with a guaranteed minimum of five years' income.

Annuity contracts cannot usually be cashed in once they have started. If they could, anyone who had bought one would endeavour to surrender it as soon as there was any sign of his health deteriorating. This the insurance company cannot allow since it depends on the profits which it makes from those who die early to pay for the losses which it makes on those who live longer than expected. It is this pooling of risk which makes the annuity so useful. It enables the insurance company to pay out a higher proportion of capital each year than would be prudent for an individual to select himself.

The main drawback with level payment annuities is, of course, the possibility of a return to high levels of inflation. Many people who bought annuities 20 years ago when they were 65 found that their income had lost two thirds of its purchasing power within little more than a decade.

The fact remains that annuities offer the highest possible continuing income. The older you are, the better will be the return and a 75 year old man could get more than £200 a year for an investment of £1,000. The time to use annuities is once a man is past 70 and a woman is over 75. Many insurance companies offer annuities which increase the amount paid out each year or two. These are generally uncompetitive since the tax free content does not rise and the initial return is greatly reduced in order to make possible the higher payouts later on.

7.9   Annuity home income schemes

It is undoubtedly true that many people invest considerable sums in their homes on the grounds that when they retire the property can be sold and part of the sale proceeds used as spending money. It is also true that many of these people eventually decide to stay in their home and consequently find their cash resources are lower than they would wish. For these people one answer to their problem is to use their home to provide spendable income and this can be done without suffering undue inconvenience. It can be achieved by arranging a home income scheme on the strength of the value that has been built up in the property. Essentially the scheme works like this:

(1)   The home owner takes a mortgage on the property up to £30,000 on an 'interest only' basis. Tax relief is gained on the interest provided that at least 90 per cent of the amount raised is used to buy an annuity.

(2)   The home owner purchases an annuity which is sufficient to cover the interest on the mortgage and leave enough over to use as spendable income.

(3)   When the home owner (or owners where there is a couple) dies the house is sold and the mortgage is repaid— the sale proceeds, less the outstanding mortgage, form part of the deceased's estate. Some protection can be obtained to cover the position if the home owner dies within a short period after setting up the plan. For example, a slightly lower annuity may be payable on the basis that part of the loan will be repaid if the person dies within the first four years.

Certain conditions must be met before such a scheme can be arranged, and generally they are applicable only to the very elderly. In the case of a single person he or she normally has to be at least 70 years of age, and a married couple must have a combined age of 150.

An an example of the level of income that can be produced, a 75 year old woman arranging a £25,000 loan would receive spendable income of about £1,400 if she pays tax at the basic rate. The scheme can be adapted to those who wish to raise some capital as well as receive an income.

Provided you are in the right age bracket and you have a property worth more than £15,000 then you could consider such a scheme. It represents a useful way of using capital 'locked away' in your home and the use of a loan in this way reduces the value of your estate for inheritance tax purposes.

8 Investment options—asset-linked

Until index-linked gilts were introduced, interest-bearing investments provided no protection against inflation. Even now, the role which they can fill is limited and they certainly do not provide any mechanism by which you can share in the increasing wealth of the country. As a result, the basis of any long-term growth investment plan must be equities (ie stocks and shares) and/or property based. During the 1970s, many observers favoured putting the greater emphasis upon property. In the last few years, the pendulum has swung back to favouring equities. This seems to be largely a reaction to the way the different types of investment have performed.

In the five years up to the end of 1990, UK equities rose by approximately 70 per cent while a typical group of properties rose by something like 50 per cent. In the five years up to the beginning of 1978, the typical share portfolio with income reinvested showed a return of only 20 per cent over the whole period, while a typical group of properties increased by 30 per cent or more.

Whether you are investing in shares or property, you will need to follow similar principles. The most important rule is to diversify your investment. This simply means not putting all your eggs in one basket. Both types of investment carry risks, and it is unnecessarily foolhardy to leave yourself completely exposed to an isolated piece of bad luck. In 1960 few shares were more highly regarded than Rolls-Royce yet this did not stop the company failing ten years later. There are many similar though less well known examples of property investments which proved equally unrewarding.

Less than 20 years ago, it was difficult for anyone except the very rich to acquire a diversified investment in a number of properties. The reason for this was simply their cost. If a person was going to buy even half a dozen properties, he had to restrict himself to comparatively small ones, and even that would have tied up several hundred thousand pounds in present day money. It is unlikely that he would want to do this, since many of the most attractive investment opportunities are in larger and more expensive property.

In contrast, the medium-sized investor had no trouble in obtaining a diversified portfolio of ordinary shares. He could put either a few hundred or few thousand pounds into each of a dozen or so companies. Alternatively, he could purchase the shares of an investment trust which itself held shares in many different companies. If he took advantage of this method of spreading his risk, he had to deal with a complicating factor. This is that the shares of investment trusts, just like those of any other company dealt with on the Stock Exchange, fluctuate in accordance with supply and demand. The result if sentiment moved against the investment trust could be for its share price to fall even though the value of the underlying securities rose. Alternatively, if demand for the trust's shares increased, their price could rise even if the underlying assets declined.

The 1960s saw the rapid expansion of the unit trust movement. This made it possible for even the smallest investor to obtain a stake in a diversified and managed portfolio of ordinary shares.

Just as unit trusts were set up to provide a ready made diversified investment in shares, property companies were set up to do the same in their field. The situation was, however, rather different since the property companies were often managed in a much more entrepreneurial way than investment trusts. They were frequently highly geared and as a result made considerable development profits. Attractive as these investments were, they were hardly a substitute for a direct stake in bricks and mortar.

8.1 Equities

Ordinary shares (or equities as they are sometimes called) are a company's risk capital; the investor who buys them expects a reasonable and rising level of dividend income and also a rise in the share price, but there is no certainty of either. If these expectations are fulfilled, then the investor is rewarded for taking the risk that the company might have encountered trading problems and that dividends might have fallen and the share price slumped. It is this risk which separates shares from other commonly held investments such as National Savings Certificates, building society shares and government stock. Where a person takes a risk with his capital he expects a higher than average return and historically this has proved to be the case.

In a recent study by stockbrokers Barclays de Zoete Wedd it is revealed that shares have given a positive real return in 43 of the last 72 years allowing for the reinvestment of gross income. Looking at returns over a much shorter period, shares would have beaten inflation if they were purchased 15, 10 and 5 years ago and gross dividends reinvested. Even when tax is taken out of the income the picture still looks attractive.

This long-term performance compares favourably with that of building society shares as the following table illustrates:

8.1.1 Table: Equity and building society funds. Net income reinvested

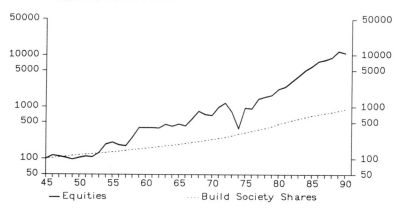

8.1.2 Table: Equity and building society funds. Net income reinvested in real terms

Source Barclays de Zoete Wedd Research Limited

Not only do shares provide capital growth, but they are also a long-term means of generating income. Dividends increased by seven per cent in real terms in 1987, the fifth successive year of real share dividend increase.

While the table shows how well shares have performed in the long term, it also clearly demonstrates what can happen to share prices during periods of economic uncertainty, as was experienced in 1974 and 1987. As mentioned in previous chapters, personal circumstances will dictate whether a *direct* investment in shares is suitable for you, but if past experience is any guide, exposure to the stock market in some form should be seriously considered by most investors, provided they can maintain their composure when stockmarkets go through a black period.

There is no reason at all why you cannot run a share portfolio yourself if you want to. Indeed, if you enjoy investment and are able to devote the time to it, then you may be lucky and do much better for yourself than you would by pooling your money with others and having it handled by professional investment managers. Despite this, investment is not an easy matter and is *extremely* time consuming if it is to be done properly. In addition, the pooled funds handled by professional managers do possess some important tax advantages and the stockbrokers' fees etc paid by the managers when changing investments are charged at a lower rate than that which applies to small investors' transactions. As a result an increasing number of people have chosen to use this route rather than handling their own portfolio.

8.2   Unit trusts

Unit trusts are designed to allow a large number of people to pool their money to buy shares. They permit existing investors to sell out and new ones to come in with no difficulty. The organisation of a unit trust is undertaken by a management company which is also responsible for choosing investments. The assets themselves are held by a trustee, who makes sure that the interests of the investors are taken care of. This structure has worked so well that there has never been a unit trust company failure, but, of course, there have been some dramatic fluctuations in unit prices in line with Stock Exchange movements of the underlying investments.

8.2.1 Example: Unit trusts

Suppose a manager collects £1 million to start a trust. It is decided that the fund is to be invested in equal amounts in two companies, both of whose shares stand at £2.

Investment in Company A: 250,000 shares @ £2
Investment in Company B: 250,000 shares @ £2
Total investment   £1,000,000

The investors between them now hold one million units @ £1 each—the precise number of units each has depends on how much they invested in the first place.

Suppose now at the next valuation, shares in company A are now £3 whereas shares in B are still £2. The total investment is now worth £1.25 million and each unit has increased in value to £1.25. If *new* investors wish to join the trust, this is the price (the offer price) at which they buy in. If existing investors wish to sell units, the manager agrees to buy them from them for a slightly lower price (the bid price). This price difference covers the costs of running the unit trust.

8.2.2 Types of fund

When unit trusts started there were only three types of fund recognised generally. These were income, general and growth funds, and corresponded to the main needs of different classes of investor. The objective of the growth fund is to seek to achieve the greatest possible capital appreciation. Managing an income fund is rather less straightforward. The object is to secure a high income for investors and some capital appreciation. It is a matter of priorities: a successful income trust will aim primarily to produce a steadily rising flow of distributions and will only be concerned with capital performance as a secondary consideration.

In a general trust, in contrast, both capital and income get equal weight. This means that the managers may accept a cut in income if this would seem likely to produce a more than commensurate improvement in the capital performance. On the other hand, they would certainly not totally disregard the interests of those who bought units in order to enjoy the distributions from them. If the income fell at one point, they would generally expect to restore it at the earliest opportunity.

Today, the situation has become much more complicated. There are now more than 1,000 different unit trusts divided into no fewer than 15 different categories.

8.2.3   Tax treatment

Disposals of investments held in unit trusts are exempt from CGT so that the managers can switch their investments without being concerned about the tax liabilities. However, you as an investor may be liable for CGT when you sell units.

Income received by the unit trust is distributed in the form of dividends. These dividends are paid out net of tax at basic rate, but the tax withheld (25 per cent) can be reclaimed if you are not liable for the tax—for example if you are able to make a repayment claim because your personal allowance exceeds your state pension and any other untaxed income that you may have. If you are a higher rate taxpayer you will have to pay some extra tax.

8.3   Investment bonds

These are lump sum investments issued by life assurance companies. They cover a broad range of investments and through them it is possible to invest in unit-linked funds invested in shares, properties, gilt-edged securities, interest-bearing investments and so on. There are also combined funds which invest in a range of different types of investment (typically a combination of property, shares and interest-bearing investments). These combined funds (or 'managed' funds as they are more commonly known) have been very popular since their introduction in the early 1970s.

The insurance company will specify the minimum initial investment which it will accept in a bond, and this is typically £1,000. Sometimes they will allow a smaller additional investment, but even then the amount is likely to be £500. The charges are similar to those levied by unit trusts, being usually a combination of an initial charge (the difference between the offer and bid price) levied when your money goes in and a recurring annual charge. Typically the initial charge is five per cent (plus a rounding amount) together with an annual management charge of 0.75 per cent per annum.

Although there is a minimum initial investment, you are normally free to make regular withdrawals from the fund even if this means that you fall below the minimum level. This is necessary because the bonds do not normally distribute the income which they earn but reinvest it within the fund. Many bonds allow you to specify how much you wish to withdraw at any one time although most of them fix a minimum withdrawal of £50. It is customary for the insurance companies to allow you to switch between one fund and another after payment of a small amount.

In structure, investment bonds are similar to unit trusts. They are 'pooled' investments and the individual investor's holding is represented by units which rise and fall in value in line with the value of the underlying investments. On the other hand, the tax treatment is completely different.

8.3.1 Tax on cashing in the bond

Gains realised on the disposal of bonds are not subject to CGT. They are, however, potentially liable to income tax.

A basic rate taxpayer who cashes in an investment bond will not normally have to pay tax on the gain. However, if you are a higher rate taxpayer, or if the gain when added to your other income lifts you into the higher tax bracket, then you will be liable to higher rate tax on the gain—but not basic rate tax.

For example, if you pay tax at a top rate of 40 per cent, then the gain will be taxed at 15 per cent (40 per cent − 25 per cent). Furthermore, a special relief known as 'top slicing' relief (see 5.2.5) may be available to reduce the tax payable—and by shrewd planning you may be able to time your disposal to avoid paying very much tax at all.

8.3.2 Partial cashing in

In the same way, if you cash in part of a bond you may be taxed at higher rates. Calculating the 'gain' in each case would be complex and so there is an agreed scheme—which offers, as a by-product, the opportunity to draw a tax free 'income'.

(1) Each year, you may withdraw up to five per cent of the *original* value of your bond without incurring any tax liability at the time.
(2) You may do this for up to 20 years (or until the total equals 100 per cent if you withdraw less than five per cent a year).
(3) You may accumulate the five per cent allowances and then make a larger withdrawal, again without any tax liability at the time (eg you could withdraw nothing for ten years and then withdraw 50 per cent).

Every time you make a partial withdrawal, the total amounts withdrawn to date are compared with the cumulative five per cent allowances. If, at any time you exceed your allowances, you will be liable for tax at higher rates on the excess and the accumulation starts all over again.

When you finally surrender the bond, the final proceeds and all the amounts you have withdrawn are added together and the overall gain is then liable to tax at the higher rates.

Therefore, bonds can play a useful part in tax planning. You can withdraw an 'income' of five per cent with no liability to tax at the time. If you finally cash in the bond when you are likely to be paying lower rates of tax (eg in retirement) you may escape a tax liability altogether. An example showing the tax calculation can be found in 6.4.1.

8.3.3   Investment bond funds

As with unit trusts, investment bonds offer the full range of funds to their investors. While most insurance companies tend to confine the choice to five or so general funds, some companies offer a far wider selection. In the main there is a choice of an equity fund (comprising mainly ordinary shares), a fixed-interest fund (investing mainly in government stocks and other interest-bearing investments), an overseas fund (which concentrates on shares quoted on foreign stock markets), a property fund and a managed fund. Of this range, the last two are arguably the most important as they are to an extent unique to insurance bonds.

8.3.4   Property funds

If you wanted to invest in property through a UK fund you had to use an insurance bond since unit trusts were not allowed to invest directly in property. However, this situation has changed and unit trusts may now invest in properties.

Just as unit trusts are invested in the shares of companies, property bonds put their money into offices, factories and other buildings. The size of property bond funds varies very greatly, with the biggest worth over £500m and some of them only a few hundred thousand pounds. This difference in size is much more significant for property bonds than it is for equity funds. There are some advantages in running a small portfolio of ordinary shares. In contrast, a large property bond fund is considerably easier to manage than a small one.

Many of the best investment opportunities involve the purchase and development of large office blocks. These cost many millions of pounds and there is no way in which they can be afforded by the small fund. In addition, the large funds have invariably got that way by growing over many years. This means that the inflow of the new money is a comparatively small proportion of the total fund. Many small funds are new and in contrast their inflow of new money is frequently a high proportion of the fund.

It can take a long time to negotiate the purchase of a property and it is difficult to judge in advance how much a property fund will have to invest. As a result, if money flows in faster than expected, a small fund may find itself with almost as much of its assets in cash as in property. This may or may not produce a reasonable investment result but it is certainly not the object of investing in a property bond. Similar considerations apply to the possibility of investors liquidating their holdings. A small property fund may maintain a higher degree of liquidity because it has a much smaller selection of properties to sell if holdings are redeemed. The alternative is for the managers to defer the redemption of these holdings until sales are completed.

8.3.5   Managed funds

Managed funds have become extremely popular in recent years and virtually every significant unit-linked insurance company offers one. Their objective is to provide an even wider spread of investment by investing in property and fixed-interest investments in addition to straightforward equity investments. The proportions of each type of investment in the fund vary according to the prevailing investment conditions of the time and the fund managers will alter the proportions as investment conditions change.

There are a variety of reasons for their popularity. Although shares can produce spectacular performance they are liable to violent fluctuation. Property is much more stable but has appreciated more slowly over the same period. Managed funds have succeeded in combining the two forms of investment. This combination of steadiness with performance is the answer for many investors. It is particularly important to avoid wide fluctuations when you may need to draw on your capital. This is the position of many retired people so that managed funds appeal particularly to them.

8.3.6   Flexibility

Investment bonds have certain features which make them very flexible. Firstly, there is a facility to 'switch' between one fund and another. For example, if you have seen your money appreciate rapidly in the equity fund and you believe it would be a good idea to capitalise on your good fortune then you can simply instruct the life assurance company to take your money out of the equity fund and put it into another fund, such as a fixed interest fund or property fund. Such a switch has no tax consequences and the company does not normally make more than a small charge for carrying out this transaction.

The switching facility means that you can vary your investment position with the added advantage that there are no income tax or capital gains tax problems as a result.

8.4   Personal Equity Plans (PEPs)

These were briefly described in 1.7.3. As an asset-linked investment their tax privileges make them one of the most advantageous investments you can buy. The sum that can be invested is relatively low, but cumulatively a married couple can create a large pool of tax free capital over a long period. One should not lose sight of the exemption of PEP income from income tax. If income of 6% is earned on the plan, this is equivalent to 10% to a top rate tax payer. As an asset-linked investment, there is every prospect that the income will grow as the years pass. Thus they offer the prospect not only of tax free capital gains, but also of a steadily rising tax free income.

8.5   Business Expansion Schemes (BES)

These were first introduced in 1981 as the Business Start Up Scheme. Its objective was to encourage investment in new business, a somewhat risky venture in most instances. For this reason full tax relief was given. It was subsequently replaced by the BES which retains many characteristics of the Business Start Up Scheme.

Some BES investments involve the subscription for shares in a single company. There are also Approved Funds where BES investors pool their money which is invested by the scheme sponsor in various enterprises. Not only is the investment fully tax deductible (up to a maximum of £40,000), but all gains arising on the investment after five years are free of personal tax. These privileges apply to both direct BES investments and investments made through an Approved Fund.

Because of the risks involved they must be classed as a very risky investment, even after allowing for the generous tax relief. Many of the companies have gone into liquidation and the BES investors have lost all their investment.

A variation of this theme was introduced in 1988 as the Assured Tenancy Scheme. This extends BES investment to residential properties which are let to tenants under the Housing Act 1988. By backing the investment with bricks and mortar a higher degree of security can be achieved. It will be some time before a proper assessment can be made of the success, or otherwise, of Assured Tenancy Schemes. Until then a cautious approach should be taken to such investment.

9 Making a Will

There are few actions which give greater benefit for less cost than the making of a Will. Despite this, many people die without making one (ie they die intestate). The result, with even the smallest estate, is to cause confusion over who should obtain Letters of Administration in order to administer it. There are also likely to be complications if the estate has to be divided under the intestacy rules. Those with substantial assets may end up paying quite unnecessary inheritance tax and, of course, it may well be that their estate is distributed in a way they do not approve of.

9.1 Intestacy

The law in Scotland is different, but in England and Wales, if you die without making a Will the intestacy rules will apply in the following way:

9.1.1 If you leave a widow(er) but no children

All your personal chattels (ie furniture, paintings, car etc) will go to your surviving spouse, who will also be entitled to the first £125,000 of the rest of your property. He or she will have a half share in the remainder of the estate. If your parents are alive they will be entitled to the rest but otherwise the half share will go to any brothers or sisters you may have or to their children.

9.1.2 If you leave a widow(er) and surviving children

Your spouse is still entitled to all your personal chattels, but he or she only gets the first £75,000 of the rest of your property. He or she then gets a life interest in one half of the remaining assets. The remainder goes to your children, who also receive the first half share when your spouse dies.

9.1.3 If you do not leave a widow(er) but you leave children or grandchildren

If there is no spouse, but you leave children the estate is divided equally between them. If one of your children dies before you, his/her children normally take the amount to which he/she would have been entitled.

9.1.4 If you do not leave a widow(er) or children

When there are neither children nor a surviving spouse, the estate passes to the parents if they are alive. If they are not, the estate passes to any brothers and sisters, or if they have pre-deceased you, then on to their children. If this does not produce an heir, the estate will pass to any surviving grandparents, or failing this will go to any aunts or uncles. If this fails to find an heir, the property will pass to the Crown. It is significant that common law wives and husbands obtain no benefit under the intestacy rules although they can apply to the court for 'reasonable provision'.

It is highly improbable that these rules will distribute your possessions in the way that you wish. Even if they do, dying intestate imposes extra burdens on your family which can be easily avoided.

9.2 A family document

When you settle down to plan your retirement is the time to decide—together, jointly—what you want to do, for yourselves and the family and for each other, when there's only one of you. Then there is a family plan about which everyone, hopefully, is happy. If not, at least they know.

In this way the Will becomes a family document which the parent can alter at any time and all interested parties have copies.

In these days your children may well be financially better off than you are, often they would rather you spent your money on yourselves than save for them.

Having decided to make a Will, it is essential to get legal advice, even if your affairs seem simple. A Will is a legal document which has to be correctly drawn up or it cannot be enforced. But more important, the law is so complicated and constantly changing that a solicitor will give good advice about how to minimise inheritance tax. Enormous savings can be made with expert advice.

9.3   The formalities

For a Will to be valid under English law, it must be signed in front of two witnesses who must sign the document themselves. Each witness should observe the other's signature as well as that of the testator. On the other hand, the witnesses are only there to witness the signature. There is no need for them to know the contents of the Will. A blind person cannot witness a Will, nor can somebody who is mentally ill. Otherwise, anyone can be a witness, although it should normally be someone over 18.

If you draw up your Will yourself, you want to be careful to choose witnesses who will not benefit under it. Any gift made to a witness, or the husband or wife of a witness, will be invalid, although this will not affect the rest of the Will. Any amendments or additions to the Will, which may be handwritten, should be signed by the testator and both witnesses in exactly the same way as the complete Will.

9.3.1   Choosing executors

One of the most important points about a Will is choosing the right executors to carry it out. The more complex your affairs, and the more elaborate your Will, the more important this is. Unfortunately, there is no straightforward answer. On the one hand, there are the executor and trustee services offered by the banks and one or two insurance companies. On the other, there is the possibility of appointing a member of the family, and in between the two lies the employment of a solicitor.

If you use a bank, you can be assured that the estate will be administered impartially, and that the technical resources will be available to deal with any complexities which may arise. However, the bank might charge around five per cent as executor for an estate worth £100,000. In contrast, a member of the family may well perform the same function for nothing.

The trouble is that Wills frequently lead to considerable ill feeling among families, and this can be greatly accentuated if the executor is not impartial. There is also the problem of finding a family member who is properly qualified to carry out the work involved if it is at all complicated. A solicitor will almost certainly charge less than a bank but the amount will vary according to the firm chosen. A small firm in the provinces is almost bound to charge less than a large London one, and will often give just as good a service. In either case you will have the advantage of impartial administration. If you know the firm well, you can also expect a more personal service than that given by a bank.

The most common solution to these problems is to appoint more than one executor. This means that you choose a solicitor, or bank or insurance company and one or two friends or members of the family. The first one can provide the technical knowledge and do the work, while the others can supply a sense of urgency and a personal interest in the case.

Although it is important that Wills should be reviewed, they are often left alone for many years. This can mean that when you die, your executors are no longer capable of administering your estate effectively. There may be little point in appointing an executor who is the same age or older than you are.

9.3.2 The importance of flexibility

It is often possible to secure considerable tax savings by writing your Will so as to take fullest advantage of the reliefs available to you. The problem is that both the tax law and the size of your estate will change. This means that you should regularly review your Will at least once a year so as to make sure that it has not become outmoded. This may be impractical and fortunately there is a better and less time consuming method. This is to leave your executors the discretion to override the dispositions you have made. They can then change the conditions of your Will so as to avoid unnecessary taxation and also to take account of any other changes in conditions which you did not foresee.

This means giving your executors the right to decide how your estate will be distributed. There are, however, a number of safeguards which ensure that this is strictly limited. Usually the Will will be in two parts. The first is quite conventional and disposes of the whole of the estate. It may well give a greater proportion of the assets to the surviving spouse than is likely to be necessary. These provisions will apply unless the executors decide to apply their discretion in the two years after the death. The second part of the Will sets out the executors' powers to override the main section. It sets out those beneficiaries to whom they can decide to distribute part of the estate. If a husband is concerned that too much may be given to other beneficiaries, he can make his widow one of the executors with a power of veto on any distributions. The same can, of course, be done by a wife who is concerned about her husband.

It is difficult to know how to divide your assets unless you know when you are going to die. If a man leaves a widow in her early sixties, he will probably want to leave her a considerable sum. She will need a house, and a sufficient income to maintain her independence. At the same time, she will want some reserves to guard her against inflation or other economic reverses over the next 20 or 30 years. If he leaves a widow in her eighties then perhaps less provision need be made.

In this case, there is every advantage in passing as many assets as possible over to a younger generation once the widow's needs have been taken care of. At the very least, it will often make sense to take advantage of the nil rate band ie the maximum amount which can be left your children without any inheritance tax (IHT) being payable.

When assets are passed over, the beneficiaries may request that these should be given to their own children. This will give rise to income which is taxable only at the rate appropriate to them, rather than being aggregated with that of their parents.

A particular advantage of this arrangement is that the executors can have up to two years to decide whether or not to exercise their powers. Any action they take is backdated to the date of death, and taxation is assessed on that basis. This can be valuable since it means that the executors are able to act on the basis of knowledge which the testator could not possibly have possessed, enabling the Will to take account of both economic changes and altered circumstances within the family. Of course, IHT is due to be paid at the normal times, so interest may have to be paid if the exercising of the executors' discretion creates a liability which is settled late. This could well be the case when the whole of the estate has been left to the widow and it is decided to divert some of the assets to other members of the family.

If this type of Will is contemplated it is essential that it is drawn up by a solicitor.

9.3.3 The alternative

If a Will has not been written on a discretionary basis, a similar effect can be achieved as a last resort if those who benefit under it agree to vary its provisions.

A 'Deed of Variation' (sometimes called a 'Deed of Family Arrangement') made within two years of death will enable a person to transfer assets with no personal IHT or CGT implications. Hence, it permits post-death planning to be made by the beneficiaries, even if the deceased did not provide for it. On the other hand, it may be more cumbersome, expensive and slightly less efficient for income tax purposes than arranging the matter through a 'discretionary' Will.

It is sometimes also possible to vary a Will by a beneficiary disclaiming a legacy. However, a disclaimer simply means that you give up your entitlement. You cannot direct that the property you have given up should fall to a particular person. The consequences will depend upon the other provisions of the Will.

9.4   Power of attorney

It is sensible for older people to give a power of attorney—a legal document to partner, older child or good friend, to manage affairs, sign cheques, etc. This can cover illness, absence or other crises.

Sadly, however, the power of attorney expires if you lose mental competence, the reason being that, because you are no longer able to be consulted or check things, greater safeguards are necessary. But, largely because of the increase in heavy treatment, the possibility of becoming a cabbage kept alive by wires and tubes in senility is growing. The Americans have introduced what is called a living Will. This is a legally binding document in which you can say, in formal terms, 'don't put me on the life support machine, keep me comfortable but don't make my hair fall out with cancer treatment and so on'.

9.5   Enduring power of attorney

In this country, we haven't gone quite as far as this but we do now have a new enduring power of attorney which continues after senility and is in many respects, legally binding and covers much the same possibilities as does a living Will in America. Not only does this allow your affairs to be managed by your attorney, but you can state how you want disease to be dealt with and it can be a relief to know what can't be done to you.

As an anxiety remover, good family Wills should be made together and related to anything that might usefully be put into an enduring power of attorney. Solicitors' fees for these are in no way near the level you read about for court work and are money very well spent. The Public Trust Office, Steward House, 24 Kingsway, London WC2B 6JX, has an excellent booklet called *Enduring Powers of Attorney* which explains all this. The Consumer Association and Age Concern also have information on such matters as Wills and enduring power of attorney and general advice about how to make the best arrangements.

9.6 Summary

If you do not make a Will, your assets will be disposed of according to the intestacy rules. Even if these broadly meet your intentions, the process is tiresome and can be protracted. There is, therefore, every reason to make a Will.

One of the most important points is the choice of the right executor or executors. There is much to be said for combining one or more members of the family with an impartial person or organisation if the estate is complex. When it comes to writing a Will, there are strong arguments in favour of making it discretionary since there may be a long period between the writing of the Will and the time when it takes effect. If the Will is not discretionary, and turns out to be inefficient for tax purposes, much can be done by post-death Deeds of Variation or disclaimers.

Once you have made your Will, lodge it with your lawyer or bank and file a copy with your personal papers, together with a note saying where the original has been placed. It is also worth appending a schedule to both copies giving details of your bank accounts, solicitors, accountant, stockbroker, life insurance policies, building society accounts, savings certificates, shares, property owned at home and abroad and any other information that will enable your executors to handle matters promptly for the beneficiaries. Allied Dunbar have a free booklet called *Arranging Your Affairs* which includes a questionnaire which will provide the required information for your executors.

Finally do not hide away the odd million in a numbered Swiss bank account without giving anybody the details. It has happened!

10   Leaving your money wisely

Inheritance tax replaced capital transfer tax (CTT) in 1986. CTT applied to virtually all lifetime gifts as well to property passing on death (subject to specific exemptions for certain types of gifts).

In this chapter we deal with the following questions:

- How is inheritance tax charged on death?
- How are lifetime gifts treated?
- What can be done to mitigate inheritance tax?

Inevitably some of what follows will seem complicated and obscure—our tax system is like that. But it is worth persevering: inheritance tax can be a heavy burden for the family of a person who ignores it altogether but it is often an *avoidable* tax. What is more, in many cases it is possible for a person to take preventive action without affecting his financial independence.

10.1   How is inheritance tax charged on death?

When a person dies, his property at the date of death and any trust property in which he has a life interest (his 'estate') is said to 'pass', ie there is a capital transfer of the value of the property. Inheritance tax is charged on this transfer. The tax is charged at 40 per cent on the value of the estate that exceeds the nil rate band (the amount exempt from tax).

£	%
0–140,000	nil
Over 140,000	40%

Bear in mind that lifetime gifts made within seven years of death may have to be taken into account in order to fix the rate of tax payable on death. So that, if you die leaving property worth £246,000 but you made chargeable transfers of £71,000 (for example) during the past year, then the IHT payable will be computed thus:

Lifetime transfers	71,000		
Estate on death	246,000		
	£317,000		
IHT on cumulative transfers of £317,000		=	70,800
Less IHT on £71,000		=	nil
IHT payable on death			£70,800

£317,000 may sound an awful lot of money, but is it? Remember that there is no special relief for your home so you can have an estate which is subject to the tax if you own a house worth £110,000 and have other assets of £31,000.

Go through the following steps to obtain an initial estimate of the tax which might be payable upon your death:

Property owned by you	£
Trust property where you have a life interest	+ £
Less property passing to your spouse	− £
Add gifts made within the last seven years	+ £
Less nil rate band (£140,000)	− £140,000
Taxable estate (taxed at 40%)	= £

In some cases it is possible to leave almost as much to the taxman as to your own family.

On the other hand, don't be too gloomy. After all, there are various exemptions such as the exemption for property passing to your spouse and the charity exemption. Furthermore, special reliefs may be available to reduce the value of certain types of unquoted shares or business property owned by you.

10.2 Main exemptions

10.2.1 Transfers to your spouse

These are totally exempt except for the rather unusual situation where the donor is domiciled in the UK but the donee is not. In that case, the exemption is limited to £55,000.

This is clearly a very important exemption as it means that generally no IHT will be payable on property which you leave to your spouse. When your widow(er) dies, however, and leaves the estate to your children, IHT is likely to apply.

10.2.2 Gifts to charities

All gifts to registered charities are exempt whether they are made during lifetime or on death.

10.2.3 Gifts for national purposes

Gifts to certain national bodies are totally exempt. These include the National Gallery, the British Museum or any similar national institution, any museum or art gallery in the UK which is maintained by a local authority or university, the National Trust, any university or university college in the UK and any local authority or Government department.

10.3 Special reliefs

10.3.1 Business property relief

A 50 per cent deduction is allowed from the value of the following property:

- a sole trader's business,
- a partner's interest in his firm,
- a controlling shareholding in a trading company,
- a holding of more than 25% of the voting shares in an *unquoted* trading company.

A 30 per cent deduction is allowed from the value of:

- property owned by a partner but used by his firm for its business,
- property owned by a controlling shareholder and used by his company for business purposes,

- smaller minority shareholdings in unquoted trading companies.

It is normally necessary for the property to have been held and for the conditions to have been satisfied for at least two years in order to qualify.

10.3.2 Agricultural property relief

A 50 per cent deduction is allowed from the value of agricultural property where:

- the owner occupied it
- a firm in which he was a partner occupied it
- the owner was entitled to obtain vacant possession within twelve months.

A 30 per cent deduction is allowed from the value of other tenanted farmland.

Agricultural relief is available only for land situated in the UK, Channel Islands or Isle of Man. The land normally has to have been owned for two years if it is occupied or seven years if it is tenanted.

10.3.3 How are lifetime gifts treated?

The main difference between IHT and CTT is that no tax is payable on property given away during a lifetime *provided*:

(1) the donor survives seven years after making the gift: *and*
(2) the gift is an outright gift by an individual to another individual and not a transfer into a trust; *or*
(3) the gift is a transfer into a special type of trust for children aged below 25 called an 'accumulation and maintenance trust' or to a trust for disabled persons; *or*
(4) the gift is a transfer to a trust where a beneficiary has an interest in possession.

Gifts which are exempt provided that the donor lives seven years are said to be 'potentially exempt transfers'. In 10.3.7 we deal with exempt gifts which are ignored even if you die within the seven year period.

10.3.4 If you die within the seven year period

The first consequence of dying within the seven years is that any potentially exempt transfers prove not to be exempt after all.

Inheritance tax is payable at a proportion of the rate in force at the time of death, the proportion being determined by 'tapering relief'. However, although the tax rates used are those in force at the date of death, the tax is charged on the original value of the gift. Another peculiarity is that when fixing the rate applicable to the gift it is necessary to take account of chargeable transfers made during the seven years preceding the gift.

10.3.5 Example: donor dying within seven years

On 1 May 1986 A gave B 100 shares in an investment company ABC Ltd. The shares had a market value of £80,000. On 27 April 1993 A dies. The shares in ABC Ltd were then worth £250,000.

The gift of £80,000 (*not* £250,000) becomes chargeable and tax would be chargeable at the rates in force at 27 April 1993. However, the IHT would take account of chargeable transfers made by A during the period May 1979–April 1986 so that if A had made chargeable transfers during that period of £120,000 the IHT on the May 1986 gift would be calculated as follows:

value of gift	£80,000
transfers made in preceding seven	
years	£120,000
	£200,000 IHT thereon = £24,000
	deduct IHT on £120,000 = £ nil
IHT on £80,000 gift before 'tapering relief'.	= £24,000

Tapering relief

Where an individual dies within seven years of making a potentially exempt transfer (PET) a proportion of the full tax is payable as follows:

Death in years	%
1–3	100
3–4	80
4–5	60
5–6	40
6–7	20
Over 7	0

As A made the gift on 1 May 1986 but died on 27 April 1993, he died within seven years of the gift being made. As he died in year seven, only 20% of the IHT is payable ie 20% of £24,000 = £4,800 payable.

A different rule is used in working out the IHT payable on the property that A owns when he dies. If A died possessed of property worth £140,000 the IHT on that property would be computed as follows:

Property passing on death	£140,000	
Gifts made in preceding		
seven years	£80,000	
	£220,000	IHT thereon = £32,000
Less notional IHT payable on chargeable		
transfers of £80,000		= nil
IHT payable on death		£32,000

The point is that the chargeable transfers made in the period of 1 May 1979–1 April 1986 are not relevant for this calculation as they occurred more than seven years before A's death.

In practice, of course, IHT would be charged at the rates in force at the date of death—we have simply used the rates currently in force for illustration.

10.3.6   Reservation of benefit

Until recently it was possible to 'give away your cake *and* eat it', ie make a gift of property which was effective for CTT purposes without giving up the income, Insurance companies produced standard arrangements intended to achieve just this ('inheritance trusts'). The replacement of CTT by IHT put an end to this and the Finance Act 1986 contained anti-avoidance provisions.

Basically, the rule is now that a gift is not effective for IHT purposes unless the donor is excluded from all benefit. If he actually enjoys some benefit, or if the gift is made in such a way that a benefit may be provided (for example, a gift is made into a discretionary trust under which the donor *could* benefit) he is said to have 'reserved benefit'. If he dies without giving up the reservation of benefit the value of the property at the date of death is included in his estate for IHT purposes. If the benefit is given up during his lifetime then he must survive a further seven years in order to avoid paying any tax.

10.3.7   Transfers which are exempt even if you don't survive for seven years

Normal expenditure out of income

There is also an exemption for gifts made out of income which are normal (ie habitual) expenditure and which do not reduce the donor's standard of living. This exemption usually covers gifts made by Deed of Covenant or premiums paid out of income to an insurance policy.

£250 exemption

There is an exemption for gifts not exceeding £250 each for any number of recipients in a tax year. The exemption is not available to cover part of a larger gift.

Annual £3,000 exemption

Lifetime gifts are exempt up to a total of £3,000 in any tax year, this limit being in addition to any gifts falling within the normal expenditure and the £250 exemptions. Both husband and wife qualify for this annual exemption. Where gifts fall short of the £3,000 limit the shortfall is carried forward to the following year and added to the allowance for that year only. Unused relief which has been carried forward from the previous year can only be utilised once the current year's annual exemption has been used.

10.3.8   Example: annual exemptions

A made potentially chargeable transfers in 1986/87 of £3,000. In 1987/88 he gave £5,000. Mrs A made transfers of £1,000 in 1985/86, £2,000 in 1986/87 and £5,000 in 1987/88.

The position is as follows:

	A	*Mrs A*
1985/86	N/A	Exempt
1986/87	Exempt	Exempt
1987/88	£2,000 potentially chargeable	£1,000 potentially chargeable

Mrs A can utilise the balance of her 1986/87 allowance against her 1987/88 transfers, but she cannot carry forward the unused amount from 1985/86.

In practice, the fact that Mr and Mrs A have exceeded their annual £3,000 exemptions may not matter—provided they live for another seven years.

Exemption for marriage gifts

There is an exemption for gifts in consideration of a marriage. The amount of the exemption depends upon the relationship of the donor to the people being married. The exemptions are as follows:

£5,000   For a parent of either party to the marriage
£2,500   By one party of the marriage to the other or by grandparents or great grandparents
£1,000   In any other case.

The gift needs to be made *in consideration* of the marriage ie prior to and conditional upon the marriage or on the occasion of the marriage. Strictly speaking the exemption is not available for gifts which are made after the marriage has already taken place.

10.4 Using a trust

For centuries trusts have been used as a means of passing capital from one person to another. In more recent times they have come to play an important role in financial and tax planning. Successive governments have sought to tax wealth that passes down on death. This has given impetus to gifting capital during lifetime, thus reducing the value of estate and, consequently, the tax paid on it.

10.4.1 What is a trust?

A trust is a means by which property is transferred by its owner (the settlor) to others (the trustees) for the benefit of third parties (the beneficiaries). Trusts can be set up during lifetime or on death through a Will (a Will trust) and are governed by the trust deed.

10.4.2 Types of trust

There are basically two types of trusts. Those that confer an immediate entitlement on the beneficiaries (interest in possession trusts) and those under which no immediate interest arises. An interest in possession trust is one where beneficiaries have the right to at least the income from the trust fund. The income may cease at some predetermined date, at which point the capital is distributed to them. Alternatively, the income can be paid to beneficiaries until they die. Usually in these cases the trust deed gives the trustees the authority to pass capital to the beneficiaries during their lifetime. On the death of the beneficiaries the trust fund reverts to other beneficiaries (known as the remaindermen).

Trusts that do not confer an immediate interest in possession are usually discretionary trusts. As the term implies, the trustees have discretion as to when and who gets the trust moneys. A key attraction of a discretionary trust is its flexibility. The beneficiaries can comprise a wide class of people, some of whom may eventually benefit, others may not. It is normal for the trust to have a defined term, at the end of which it is wound up and the assets distributed. Further uses for discretionary trusts are described later.

10.4.3   Accumulation and maintenance trusts

It is worth making a special mention of this type of trust. An A & M settlement, as they are called, has special tax privileges. Their use is confined to beneficiaries under the age of 25 and accordingly are suited as a means of providing for minor children.

10.4.4   Benefits

Trusts have two advantages. Firstly, the creation of a trust usually reduces the size of the settlor's estate by the value of the trust assets. This reduces the value of an estate on death and thus saves inheritance tax. What is more, all the appreciation on the asset from the time the gift is made to the date of death falls outside the estate. And secondly, because the assets are held by trustees for the beneficiaries, a trust is a means of controlling the way capital is used for other, perhaps less responsible, people.

Income tax and capital gains tax can also be saved as a trust is a separate tax entity. It pays income and capital gains in the same way as an individual, although the tax rates and allowances are somewhat different. Nevertheless, the rate of income tax paid on the trust income should be lower than that paid by the settlor. A trust also has its own CGT annual allowance.

10.4.5   Role of the trustee

A dictionary definition of a trustee is a person to whom the legal title to property is entrusted to hold or use for another's benefit. A trustee has a responsibility to ensure the trust funds are used in the best interests of the beneficiaries and carry out the terms and conditions of the trust deed. In the case of a discretionary trust, it is the trustees who decide who benefits and to what extent. This is a responsible task, and beneficiaries can take legal action against the trustees to protect their interests. It is possible for the settlor to be a trustee, thus retaining some direction over the trust moneys. Additional trustees will also be appointed, and one would normally be a professional person such as a solicitor or an accountant.

10.4.6   Gifts into trust

Lifetime gifts to trusts other than those previously mentioned are chargeable at the time of the gift whether or not the donor survives seven years. Inheritance tax is payable at 50 per cent of the normal rates but further tax could be payable if he dies within the following seven years.

10.4.7   What can you afford to give away?

Your first priority must be to ensure that you and your spouse will continue to have sufficient income to meet your needs. No-one should expect you to beggar yourself in order to save IHT which may not be payable for ten or twenty years. If your heirs *do* expect you to make substantial sacrifices they almost certanly don't deserve it. You also need to ensure that your widow(er) will have sufficient income to be financially independent when you have passed on.

Do be cautious

You should make some allowance for future inflation. We all know people who were comfortably off when they first retired, but who now have to watch their spending more carefully. As you get older you may need to draw on capital in order to cover medical and nursing bills.

Let's first examine the aspects that should be considered before you make any large gift:

- Can you afford to make this gift?
- Will the recipient use it wisely?
- Should you defer making the gift?
- Is there a time limit in which you must make up your mind?
- Can it be passed on equally well by your Will?
- Is it better to give money or property?
- Can/should any strings be attached?
- Are there any other taxes to be considered?

. . . but don't give up

Even if you feel unable to make large gifts at the present time there is generally still a great deal that can be achieved by careful planning.

Basic strategy

Inheritance tax can be substantially alleviated by a combination of the following straightforward methods:

- funding for the potential liability via insurance,
- making use of the annual exemptions,
- taking advantage of the seven year rule by setting up discretionary trusts,
- drawing up an appropriate Will,
- equalising your estates,
- putting all or part of any property you inherit into trust.

10.5 Funding the tax

Some people have sufficient disposable income to enable them to take out insurance which completely covers their inheritance tax liability. This is often not that expensive if you start taking out policies before you get too old, say in your 50s or early 60s. On the other hand a lot of people consciously decide that they will not try to cover all the tax payable on their deaths but do decide to take out some insurance. It's a fine thing for a family if you can afford to go all the way but this attitude is perfectly understandable. It's a question of priorities. However, the point to recognise is that some insurance is generally thought to be most desirable, if not essential.

How do you work out the level of cover that is needed? This must vary according to your circumstances, but it may be helpful if we tell you how many people approach this matter. We have all heard people say that what really concerns them is that their children will have to sell the family home or other assets which have been in the family for many years. Similarly, where a person has spent his life building up a business or family company he naturally hates the thought of his life's work being sold because money for death duties cannot be found in any other way. In other words, those people regard insurance as a way of ensuring that their heirs can afford to retain certain property.

Some people look at matters slightly differently. They are anxious to avoid a situation where executors have to sell assets in a poor market to meet IHT. We hear them say that their children will be much better off than they were at that stage in their own lives, even after the taxman has taken his slice. They have no particular inclination to stint themselves just in order to pass over even more but they do feel they want to make a contribution to give their family a financial 'breathing space'. What must be remembered is that, when a person dies, it is necessary in most cases for a grant of representation to be obtained by the executors or administrators of the estate. This enables them to deal in the assets and distribute the estate to the beneficiaries. In order to obtain a grant it will be necessary to produce, amongst other things, a return of the whole estate for inheritance tax. If inheritance tax is payable then this must be paid in full or in part before a grant can be issued. Usually money can be borrowed to pay the tax and, once the grant is obtained, assets are sold to repay the loan. A point to remember is that in many cases the assets are shares or residential property and the price they fetch depends upon market conditions at the time. Unfortunately there is no guarantee that a good price, or indeed any price, can be obtained. In October 1987 share prices were very low. In 1990 it was almost impossible to sell residential property, even after dramatic reductions in the value. Forced sales during depressed markets can mean that beneficiaries lose out on the full value of their inheritance.

This is where adequate insurance can be so valuable. It provides liquidity exactly when it is needed. Beneficiaries can use the policy moneys to pay the tax and then hold onto their inheritance and sell the property when it will fetch a good price.

10.6   Important considerations

10.6.1   Which type of policy?

Whichever category you fall into, you should get some quotes. You know what you can afford to pay without suffering hardship; ask for details of the cover that this will provide on a whole life basis.

Think about the effects of the way that you have drawn your Will. If most of the joint estate will pass to the survivor of you and your spouse, the inheritance tax will actually be payable on the death of the second of you to die. In that case a Joint Life Last Survivor policy may be appropriate. This is a policy where the insurance company pays out on the death of the survivor—ie when both you *and* your spouse have died. The premiums are bound to be cheaper than separate policies on each individual life, and the money will arrive when it is really needed—and not before.

Insurance companies can be flexible. Their business is providing a range of standard products which meet people's requirements. Some policies may fit your requirements better than others. For example, most quotes will show a premium calculated on the basis that it will be payable until both you and your spouse have died. On the other hand, you may feel it is unfair to saddle your spouse with the burden of paying heavy annual premiums. If that is how you look at it you should get quotes for a Joint Life Last Survivor policy where the premiums stop on the first death. Similarly, you may anticipate that after (say) ten years you may find the premiums a strain on your finances. Don't be put off, some unit linked policies are designed with this option in mind.

10.6.2   Setting up the policy in a tax efficient way

You also need to consider how the policy should be owned. In many cases it will be best for it to be 'written in trust' so that inheritance tax is not charged on the proceeds when the insurance company pays out.

10.6.3   Take advice on insurance matters

Insurance is a technical field and you need to take advice from an expert, someone who is thoroughly conversant with all the various aspects of different policies and who has been trained to be able to select those policies which are appropriate in your particular circumstances. If you deal with a company representative make sure that the company has adequate resources and personnel at head office to provide the necessary technical support for their representatives.

10.6.4   Making use of the £3,000 exemption

Substantial sums may be transferred by making full use of this exemption. A common means of using the annual exemption is to fund a life policy which will cover a large part of the eventual IHT liability.

10.6.5   Example: the £3,000 exemption

A and his wife are aged 60 and 55 respectively. There is a potential liability of IHT of £100,000 which will arise on the second death. A decides to cover this liability by effecting an insurance policy for the benefit of his children.

An annual premium of approximately £1,270 will be required. This would normally be exempt under the £3,000 annual exemption (or the 'normal expenditure' exemption) and that the policy proceeds of £100,000 would be completely tax free.

If A died after ten years and Mrs A did not wish to continue paying premiums, the £100,000 cover could remain in force for another 14 years—although the policy's surrender value would gradually diminish if this option were taken.

These policies obviously become more expensive the longer you leave them, but not necessarily prohibitively expensive. The premium for a man aged 65 and wife aged 61 would normally be around £1,850 per annum and if you are 70 and 65 when you start, the premiums would still only be of the order of £2,700 per annum.

However, the premiums may have to be 'weighted' if you are in poor health when you take out the policy.

10.7   Capital gains tax savings

Another possibility is to use an important CGT relief. It is possible for a person to make a gift into a discretionary trust of shares or securities on which there is a substantial unrealised capital gain and for a joint election to be made so that the capital gain is 'held over'. In other words, for CGT purposes these shares are deemed to be transferred at their original cost.

The trust will have its own CGT annual exemption and it may be possible to realise the profits over a number of years without incurring CGT.

One situation where this could prove useful is where an employee has acquired significant shares through an approved share option scheme. Often the base cost of the shares is very low and consequently the gain is substantial.

Another strategy is for the shareholder to pass the shares on death to the surviving spouse. The transfer is exempt from IHT and CGT. What is more the base cost is uplifted to the market value at the date of death. The spouse can then make an outright gift, or set up a trust, without worrying about CGT.

10.7.1   Taking advantage of the seven year rule

If tax saving is the main consideration, and a person is sufficiently wealthy, it clearly makes sense to give away the nil rate band every seven years. Expressed in another way, all other things being equal, it makes sense for older people to make a transfer of capital as soon as they feel comfortable in doing so, in order to start the seven year period running. Provided that they survive seven years, the gift will be exempt and the individual will have back his nil rate band intact.

The problem which applies for most of us is that we cannot afford to give away as much as the nil rate band. Furthermore, there is the future to be borne in mind—it may be that our widow/widower will need more capital that we can foresee, inflation may go up again and so on. Also we may not be sure which members of our families we wish to have our capital, we may be concerned that having too much capital at a relatively early age will spoil their character, tempt them into extravagance or the wrong sort of company and so on. Therefore, however, it might make sense *in theory*, from a tax planning point of view, to give away the nil rate band every seven years, there will very often be good reasons for not wishing to make outright gifts.

A possible solution is to make a discretionary settlement or trust where no one beneficiary has an entitlement to income, but the trustees have discretionary powers to pay income (or capital) to any one of a class of beneficiaries. In practice, the class of beneficiaries can be quite small and could be limited to your immediate family. This can be an effective way of saving inheritance tax whilst retaining flexibility and a measure of control. We have previously mentioned the anti-avoidance rule where the donor reserves a benefit, but there is nothing to stop him just being a trustee of such a trust.

The one chink in this seemingly impenetrable obstacle is that it is only the *donor* who must be totally excluded, the spouse may be able to benefit. One way of taking advantage of this is to put property into a discretionary trust where the trustees can pay sums to any one of a range of beneficiaries including your spouse. Or it may be appropriate for your spouse to set up a trust which includes you as a beneficiary. Be careful and take advice, there are further anti-avoidance provisions which need to be negotiated if you wish to make use of this possibility. Including your spouse is very much something you should regard as a final fall-back provision in case your circumstances should alter radically.

In any event, forming a discretionary trust of this nature is certainly not a panacea since inheritance tax will be payable on the creation of the trust if it takes you over the IHT threshold or on paying benefits out of the trust in future.

Insurance

It is often possible to effect seven year insurance on very reasonable terms to ensure that your family will be in funds to pay any extra IHT which may be payable if you fail to survive the seven year period.

10.7.2 Example of possible saving

B has a portfolio worth £150,000. If he puts shares worth £30,000 into trusts he may save IHT of up to £12,000 (depending on the total size of his estate) provided that he survives seven years. Furthermore, IHT will not be charged on any capital growth in the shares he has given away so that if these shares were worth £60,000 after five years, a further saving of IHT will have been achieved. The capital growth will accrue outside B's estate and will escape IHT on B's death even if B does not survive the seven year period.

Costs

A firm of solicitors will need to be involved to draw up the trust deed. In practice their fees should normally be within the range of

£400–£750. Capital gains tax may not be payable on the transfer of securities to the trustees provided that the trustees are resident in the UK (the hold-over provisions apply to gifts to certain trusts).

10.8 Drawing up your Will to minimise IHT

We have already mentioned the practical advantage of leaving part of the estate in a discretionary trust. This was basically recommended in order to use the provision which allows trustees to make appointments within two years of the death and have those payments treated as if they had been contained in the Will. There can, however, also be an advantage in property remaining within a discretionary trust after the two year period has elapsed. A discretionary Will trust can be a way of enabling income and capital to be made available to your spouse whilst making use of your nil rate band on your death.

10.8.1 Example: discretionary Will trust

A dies leaving a 65 year old widow and an estate of £330,000. If he leaves his entire estate to Mrs A and she dies five years later the IHT position will be:

IHT on A's death	nil	(covered by spouse exemption)
IHT on Mrs A's death	£76,000	(ie IHT on £330,000)

If A had left Mrs A £220,000 and had left £110,000 in a discretionary Will trust then her income might have been virtually no different. She would have received the income on the £220,000 left to her outright and the trustees of the Will trust might well have paid most of their income to her. However, from an IHT point of view there would be a considerable improvement. The property held in the discretionary Will trust would not form part of Mrs A's estate on her death so the IHT position would be:

IHT on Mr A's death	nil	(covered by nil rate band and spouse exemption)
IHT on Mrs A's death	£32,000	(IHT on £220,000)
	£32,000	

Once again, do bear in mind that you can appoint your widow as a trustee through your Will and this will give her a greater sense of security in that she can expect to receive the income from the discretionary Will trust.

10.8.2 Equalising your estates

Provided it does not conflict with personal considerations, it makes sense to arrange matters so that your own and your wife's estates are roughly the same value (ie 'equalised'). The point is that your Wills can then be drawn up so as to minimise IHT if some catastrophe should strike you both in rapid succession. Another point to bear in mind is that you do not know who is going to die first.

The need for this can be shown by the following example:

10.8.3 Example: equalisation

B and Mrs B have a joint estate of £360,000. However, it is divided unevenly with B owning property worth £330,000 and Mrs B £30,000. If Mrs B dies first and B dies shortly afterwards IHT of up to £76,000 could be payable.

If their estates had been equalised and Mr & Mrs B's Wills had contained 'survivorship' clauses so that property passed to the survivor only if he/she survived six months, the total IHT would have been only £32,000.

10.8.4 Putting property you inherit into trust

You may be a beneficiary under a relative's Will or you may be a beneficiary under a family trust. Perhaps your father created a Will trust and you recently became entitled to the fund on your mother's death. The question is whether you should merge your inheritance with your own assets or pass it over to your children etc. Tax experts refer to this as 'generation skipping' and it certainly makes sense on paper provided you feel comfortable about 'handing over what you have never had'.

Provided that action is taken in time it is possible to make an exempt gift of such an inheritance. Furthermore, the gift can be exempt right away: you do not have to survive for seven years. However, the technical and legal aspects need to be handled carefully: this is a 'classic' situation where taking professional advice at an early stage is likely to pay dividends.

10.8.5   Example: IHT planning in action

Let's take a look at the savings that can be achieved by taking quite simple steps at the right time.

Before

Harold and Mary are aged 63 and 58 respectively. They own the following property:

	Harold £	Mary £
Chequers (their home)	100,000	(joint)
Stocks and shares	70,000	30,000
Cash deposits	20,000	30,000

Harold's Will leaves everything to Mary (and vice versa). On their death they want their property to be divided equally amongst their son and daughters.

Harold and Mary's income position is:

	Harold £	Mary £
Pension (index linked)	15,000	–
Dividends	3,500	1,500
Interest	1,400	2,000
	19,900	3,500
less income tax	3,721	51
net income	16,179	3,449

In fact they live off Harold's pension. From time to time Mary draws on her deposits but Harold's investment income is reinvested. In two years they will become entitled to the State Retirement Pension.

At present inheritance tax would be payable only when they have both died. The inheritance tax on their combined wealth of £250,000 would be £44,000. However, if they continue to re-invest surplus income they may well be worth £300,000 by the time that Harold is 70. The inheritance tax could then be £64,000. The children could, therefore, expect to receive the equivalent of £206,000 in due course.

After

Harold and Mary changed their Wills. Harold's Will provides that £50,000 of his stocks and shares should go into a discretionary will trust under which Mary will benefit. The balance of his estates passes to her absolutely. Mary's Will now provides for her assets to pass directly to their children if she dies before Harold.

They decide to start giving away part of Harold's investment income. After tax he gets £3,675 per annum. Harold and Mary allocated £2,500 for gifts (they will vary the allocation according to circumstances). £1,000 per annum is to go into a Joint Life Last Survivor Policy (written in trust for the children) which should produce about £61,500 on the second death.

Harold and Mary's children will, therefore, get

	£
From lifetime gifts (£2,500 per annum, say)	25,000*
From insurance policy	61,500
Harold's Will Trust	50,000
Mary's estate on her death	200,000
less inheritance tax	2,400
	312,500

It is an increase of nearly half.

* Obviously this depends on how long Harold and Mary live—and whether they continue to make annual gifts at this level.

Further reading

Allied Dunbar Money Guide *Leaving Your Money Wisely* by Tony Foreman.

11 Accommodation in retirement

by Bill Loving

Bill Loving was the founder-editor of Choice *magazine. Now retired, he continues to write and lecture on various aspects of retirement planning.*

The retirement home, rather like retirement itself, is a fairly modern invention. As a term, it is not to be solely identified with grouped dwellings for the elderly, which are equipped with a warden and alarm systems useful in emergencies. Such dwellings are a form of retirement housing, but make up only one aspect of a many-sided subject.

11.1 A retirement home

In the context of this book, a retirement home is one which has been designed or adapted to meet the retirement needs of an individual. Retirement these days embraces an age group which reaches from the middle-fifties to the nineties or more. Such a vast range means that there is an enormous variety of people and backgrounds, with persons having quite different ideas on what constitutes for them the most suitable type of retirement abode. Older men and women make up a substantial part of the national community and, like younger ones, differ widely in tastes, health, income, expectations and lifestyle. It therefore follows that there is no one general standard model of a retirement dwelling. It also follows that the term itself can apply to a spacious house as well as to a small flat, or anything between.

For anyone sorting out his housing needs in retirement, there are at least three common factors which apply. The purpose here is to outline these and then, in the following sections, to discuss various options.

Factor one is actually to engage in some hard thinking in advance about the shape, size and location of the retirement home. Such thinking will be coloured to a large extent by what retirement means to a person. On the whole, most people appreciate that retirement can last a long time and that it is a period of life which, in this day and age, far from being a rundown to the grave, can be viewed as a period of positive growth and achievement.

The second factor inevitably brings into play the question: Will the kind of home that is ideal for my retirement in, say, my early sixties, continue to be just as good a proposition in another twenty years' time?

The third factor applies to those sharing a home. Sooner or later there will remain just one survivor of a partnership and, statistically speaking, the odds are that the husband is more likely to predecease the wife. What effect should this have on one's planning especially when it is remembered that a home which is perfectly capable of being managed by a couple may become a wearisome and expensive burden to someone left alone?

How far these points should influence a decision on retirement accommodation is strictly for the individual, but some guidelines may suggest themselves in the rest of the chapter.

11.2   Moving or staying?

To move on or to say put? On the whole, orthodox advice from organisations engaged in the housing field for the elderly, sounds almost a negative note. This is understandable enough because most are dealing with aged people whose health and mobility are on the wane. Even if a move has to be made, the received opinion is that it is better to settle in new quarters in the known and familiar neighbour-hood rather than to venture into alien tertitory.

However, if there is an awareness that an option is to play safe, is there not also room for a touch of optimism?

Planning a retirement home must relate to the needs of the people involved. A prudent couple in their sixties may abandon a large house and an equally large garden for a two-bedroom flat in a sheltered housing scheme on the basis that this is an insurance against reaching the eighties and not then being so spry.

There is an obvious logic on their side, but no more than, say, another pair who decide to remain in a sizeable establishment because it has always been their home. The family may have departed, but the fact that they have reached retirement does not constitute a reason for sacrificing space. These are two extremes, but there are some general pointers that may be worth examining.

Any retirement accommodation should be so arranged that it is easy and convenient to run (this applies, of course, to other households, whatever the age group). If a decision is taken to stay on in the present home, there is a case for seeing how suitable it is for retirement. Can it be re-arranged in ways that equate with growing older?

There is the perfectly true story of one enthusiast given the task of planning his home for retirement who suggested that one should begin by trying to envisage everything likely to go wrong during later years and then equip the premises accordingly.

If, for instance, a long illness or some disability was a likely possibility, was there a downstairs room which could be switched to use as a bedroom? Indeed, were there facilities to live without undue strain on the ground floor?

His list included items such as easy access to garden and house; a kitchen with cupboards within painless reach, and with undemanding equipment and storage; and home heating and insulation of a high standard.

He also favoured lighting of a kind that abolished dark patches; grab rails in the toilet and bathrooms; the installation of taps of the lever variety; a good security system for doors and windows, particularly the front door through which visitors could be inspected before admittance; and—back to the garden again—the area planted and laid out in such a way that it was no longer quite so labour-intensive.

A healthy and vigorous person, contemplating his forthcoming retirement, may well blench at the prospect of converting his home into the equivalent of a nursing home for his old age. But without going the whole hog, there is a case for being satisfied that the home can be adapted, even if only on a gradual stage-by-stage basis, to meet changing needs. In a sense, it is all part of the business of standing back, figuratively speaking, and taking a long-term look at this particular area.

A virtue of moving (admittedly few would see it in this light at first) is that one is forced ruthlessly to assess anew the worth of all the bits and pieces that have accumulated during a lifetime of work and family domesticity. Attics and spare rooms are often full of articles stowed away years ago and rarely touched since. In the old home so much lumber is taken for granted and it is sometimes quite a shock to realise when organising a removal, usually into less spacious premises, that there has to be a wholesale clear out.

The discipline of having to perform major surgery on one's possessions is escaped by those who stay put. Yet it can be argued that a large part of the cherished clutter of many years can constitute an unnecessary burden as one grows older. To those who remain anchored in the old neighbourhood is it unreasonable to suggest that as part of the process of preparing the home for retirement they, too, should look anew at their accommodation and all it holds?

11.3 Finding a new home

Housing mobility among retired people is still confined to a minority, but it is a large minority, especially among home owners, and present trends indicate that it is increasing. A spur to the rising graph is the development of what could be called two-stage retirement home progress. People who initially settled in a dwelling envisaged as good enough to see them through their retirement, often find as they grow older that it is better to move on to a more suitable abode. The move is not necessarily caused by frailty or infirmity. Quite frequently it stems from the actual experience of some years of retirement and the recognition that the moment has arrived for re-thinking the current position.

In general, most people on retirement move within a radius of thirty or forty miles of their old surroundings. The factors which decide a move to a new area are many and various. Sheer economics could play a major part. Selling a large property and buying a smaller one could release a sizeable amount of capital and also lead to lower maintenance and domestic costs. Successful trading down obviously depends on geography. Selling a house up north and buying one down south is not likely to be financially profitable. In reverse, there could be a windfall. Even shifting out of expensive London into slightly less expensive areas south, east and west of the capital, could mean an addition to one's bank balance.

But economics are not usually the ruling factor in going elsewhere. The family home, chosen because of schools and access to work, may be in an environment which has ceased to appeal. Much is made in the to-move-or-stay debate of the possible isolation and loneliness that may result if one shifts away. But local communities are highly mobile and always changing. The nearness of married sons and daughters and their families, for instance, may be a tug, but offspring often have to move themselves in compliance with the demands of their employment.

In selecting a new location, some suggestions can be made. It is fair to assume that if a person is accustomed to the facilities and amenities of an urban life, it is an elementary precaution to check on what a prospective location may have to offer in this respect. Are there local organisations that can cater for retirement interests? What provision is there for recreation? Is the shopping well sited and, preferably, within easy walking distance? How good (or poor) are the various public services such as libraries, adult education facilities, hospitals, dentists, theatres, restaurants, pubs and clubs?

There is, too, an assessment to be made of road and rail communications. A small test is to imagine living car-less in the area. What will replace the service that a car provides? Local bus services should be studied. If a railway station is within easy distance, this is a plus and better still if it is on a main line.

The test over, and with, the car again, is how accessible is the area to the outside world? Few want to live close to a motorway, but being within reasonable distance of one has much to commend it.

Finally, having to put down fresh roots in a new community is not always the hazardous operation that it is often portrayed as being. It is useful if one already has contacts in the area, but even arriving as a complete newcomer re-settlement need not pose a threat. People who have had to move frequently in the course of their working lives are better at it than others because they learn from experience of the need to reach out and mix.

Interests and hobbies which involve meeting others are helpful— hence the need to check on what a new location has to offer. There also has to be a recognition that the onus is on the fresh arrival to make the first move and to be outgoing. It is not much use sitting at home and waiting for callers.

On the whole, the average person should not find it difficult to cease feeling like a stranger, providing he makes the effort to go a handsome half way.

11.4 Life on the level—a flat or bungalow

The point of similarity between a flat and a bungalow is that the accommodation is normally arranged on one floor. Otherwise they are vastly different. A flat, unless it is on the ground floor, has to be reached by stairs, which is an argument for making sure that a lift is installed.

Living on one level is less demanding in basic living terms than occupying a two-storeyed house. Whether or not this is a major requirement depends on the individual and his or her particular retirement needs. All one can do is to present some of the main advantages and disadvantages and leave the decision-making to the person concerned.

As a starter, a flat usually means freedom from the care of a garden. External maintenance is, as a rule, a responsibility included in a service charge which is likely to take care of the cleaning and decorating of halls, stairways and other common areas, care of the grounds and insurance of the buildings as well.

There may be a covenant forbidding the keeping of pets; and for those who like do-it-yourself activities a home workshop, however unambitious, may not be possible. Immediate neighbourhood noise can be an affliction, although decibel intrusion is not just confined to flats.

Flats are mostly leasehold from 99 to 999 years, with the leaseholder paying ground rent. Leases with less than 80 years to run may not be so attractive. Flats tend to be compact, which means that they cost less to run and heat and are not burdensome to look after. The disadvantages could include sheer lack of space. Whether life is lonelier in a flat than in a house is an issue which does not admit of rational discussion. So much depends upon the individual and the pulse of his social and outside life.

As for bungalows they come with a garden and, if detached, with a moderately broad strip of ground. Like flats, well designed bungalows make for efficiency in running. Intelligent planning of the garden, with patio, paving and other landscaping can be introduced to save labour. Once more this can be a gradual process. The man who likes a fine stretch of lawn, a display of annuals, a kitchen garden and a greenhouse, can lessen the chores as he thinks fit.

It is always worth mentioning that flats or bungalows frequently offer accommodation suitable for a couple, but which may prove cramped when visitors come to stay, particularly married offspring with children. The adequate accommodation of such welcome guests, if calculated in the number of spare bedrooms required, might logically preclude a move to a smaller home. Here, priorities have to be sorted out. A couple seeking a retirement home are wise to consider their own housing needs before anything else. After all, sons and daughters and grandchildren can usually be 'squeezed in' on short stays and to plan otherwise is to acquire accommodation that may be grossly under-used.

11.5 Mobile homes

A form of housing often overlooked is the mobile home, once, years ago, regarded as a caravan and a rather inferior type of dwelling. For many people the image remains yet, desite the fact that the caravans of yesteryear have evolved into well appointed units, linked to all the normal main services, water, gas, electricity, drains—and which bear comparison in every respect with two, three or four bedroom bungalows.

The two main criticisms are that:

- unlike a normal dwelling, the capital value shrinks steadily, and
- the materials used are not as durable as bricks and mortar. In consequence the 'life' of a unit is strictly limited.

Those in the mobile home industry say such strictures are a left-over from the days when a caravan was adapted to form a static home, that modern materials compare favourably with those used in conventional buildings, and that in recent years mobile homes have appreciated in value.

Anyone investigating should satisfy himself on a large number of points, including not only charges for services and the provision of amenities on the site itself, but also the availability of essential facilities in the surrounding districts.

11.6 Sheltered and not-so-sheltered housing

Sheltered housing is usually explained as grouped housing for elderly people who, while living their own independent life in their own self-contained units, may be vulnerable because of their age and require some degree of care supplied by a warden. The warden's job is to keep an unobtrusive and friendly eye on residents and to respond to an emergency signal for help.

A transformation has taken place in the sheltered housing schemes available. The main influence at work is the private construction industry. Builders have discovered that a new and expanding market for the supply of purpose-built dwellings for retired people, normally home owners, has come into existence.

In the past, home owners received a low priority in qualifying for this form of housing. Local authorities and housing associations, often in co-operation, supplied accommodation on a rental basis for council tenants and for those with insufficient capital to provide a roof of their own. Today, thanks to the builders, there are innumerable developments of grouped housing available to anyone, normally on a leasehold basis. All levels of the market are catered for. Schemes embrace luxury flats in country houses, village-type retirement communities and purpose-built blocks of flats. Grouped housing can also be made up of a mix of dwellings—flats, bungalows and, in some cases, three and even four bedroom houses. Basically, the emphasis is on accommodation providing one or two bedrooms.

Although the appeal is to the older-retired, there are increasing numbers of the younger-retired who are beginning to opt for this form of housing. To widen the appeal to the younger age-group, who may mentally classify such housing as fit for only the really old, the sales line is changing. Increasingly the message is that here is a trouble-free home, where one can get on with enjoying an active retirement, with the assurance that the accommodation is eminently suitable not only now but when one grows older.

The process has often led to the warden becoming the secretary, the administrator or just the housekeeper. Indeed, in some cases, she has vanished entirely and the alarm system is linked to a central outside panel, under constant monitoring. The very word 'shelter' is becoming taboo; there is a marked preference for 'retirement home' and the premises are presented as units sensibly equipped to meet the needs of retirement.

It should be mentioned, in passing, that some builders in planning new estates open to all age groups are offering dwellings specifically for retired people which, they say, give the opportunity of living in a 'mixed' community. Such accommodation does not come under the heading of 'sheltered'.

Anyone interested in grouped housing should be satisfied on a number of points. Is the property freely marketable—provided that the purchaser is of the requisite age? (The age of entry to retirement homes is usually from fifty-five or sixty upwards.) Does the leaseholder retain the right to sell the residence himself and what proceeds, if any, are deducted from the selling price? Is there an obligation to contribute towards a sinking fund for major repairs? The length of lease and the amount of ground rent should be clearly set out.

The service charge generally covers all outside repairs and maintenance, the upkeep of the gardens, estate lighting, property insurance and maintenance of the alarm system, as well as the cost of warden service. Ask if there are any extra costs and check on arrangements for increasing the charge.

Entry phones on all communal entrances are regarded as essential. The kind of management also requires scrutiny. Builders often enter into an agreement with a housing association so that the latter becomes responsible for the administration and running of a scheme. Such organisations have had a long experience of specialised housing for older people and the link is of mutual benefit.

Finally, it is as well to be sure that the scheme is in a desirable area, with easy access to amenities and services.

11.7   Sources of further information

For straightforward house hunting in a particular area, apart from the round of estate agents in the locality, a study of both the editorial and advertising columns of the local press over some weeks gives a useful picture of the district. Lists of local organisations, recreational facilities and much similar information should be available from the public library or the town hall. A Citizens' Advice Bureau is also helpful.

For more about mobile homes, the Department of the Environment issues a free booklet entitled *Mobile Homes—A Guide For Residents and Site Owners*, which answers many queries.

There is also a publication which specialises in this particular subject and which provides a useful reader service: *Mobile Homes and Holiday Caravan*, Link House, Dingwall Avenue, Croydon CR9 2TA.

As a follow up to the section on sheltered and not-so-sheltered housing a list of builders engaged in the retirement housing market is obtainable free from New Homes Marketing Board, 82 Cavendish Street, London W1M 8AD.

The Housing Information Department, Age Concern, 60 Pitcairn Road, Mitcham, Surrey CR4 3LL issues a *Buyer's Guide To Sheltered Housing*. Age Concern also supplies information on housing provided by local authorities and housing associations.

Local housing information—housing association and private sector projects as well as residential homes—is obtainable from the local authority. Lists of housing associations on a regional basis are available from the Housing Corporation, Maple House, 149 Tottenham Court Road, London W1P 0BN.

For people who become incapable of living an independent life, through physical or mental infirmity, homes are provided by local authorities, by voluntary associations, by some housing associations and charities and by owners of private accommodation.

Much depends on personal and financial circumstances, but the social service department of a local authority can give detailed information covering a particular area and Age Concern also can supply guidance.

An interesting and fairly recent development in this connection in both the commercial and charitable field has been the concept of 'total care' facilities. The Abbeyfield Society, for example, is making facilities available so that when a member of one of their homes is unable to remain independent he can be transferred to a 'care' or nursing home unit. A large private builder, McCarthy and Stone, Ltd, which specialises entirely in sheltered housing, is also offering facilities of an hotel character, where people can be provided with full or partial nursing and support services.

12 Leisure activities and pastimes

by Bill Tadd

So, how are you going to use, not simply fill, those 2,000 hours each year that until retirement were taken up by work? Life must have purpose if it is to be enjoyed to the full. Our jobs provide more than income. They establish a routine and give us a sense of identity, the companionship of colleagues, physical exercise and mental stimulation. All must be replaced.

The swiftest route to decline and domestic discord is that followed by the man who embarks on an undisciplined retirement of total relaxation. He ends up under his wife's feet; she begins to feel she is a domestic servant rather than a partner and soon the stress of work is replaced by the more unhealthy stress of frustration.

12.1 Planning your activities

Surveys taken over a number of years by the Pre-Retirement Association demonstrate that the main worry of those approaching retirement is, quite understandably, their financial situation. After retirement, this spectre fades significantly and is replaced for some by the realities of loneliness, boredom, lack of incentive. Some actually complain of the absence of 'stress'.

Fortunately, the same surveys also show that the great majority of men and women make the transition successfully and really do regard retirement as a new life to be enjoyed, one in which they have total control—perhaps for the first time. But these are people who have given thought to the matter in advance and have planned not just their finances but also their activities.

Leisure means time to do what pleases you. Perhaps you have a hobby or pastime and you cannot wait to devote all your energy to it. That could be a mistake. A life spent on the golf course or the bowling green is healthy for the body but does little to exercise the brain although the social contact these sports provide must not be under-valued.

12.2   Togetherness

It is delightful when married couples have identical interests, but you can have too much of a good thing. You are individuals as well as partners and should try to develop at least one interest or activity on your own account. Whether one or both went out to work you are accustomed to leading separate existences for much of the week. Retirement brings you together for long periods, sometimes uncomfortably long.

A common mistake is for the husband to decide to spend some of his leisure time taking an interest in the running of the home. The last thing his wife wants is his managerial skills intruding into her domain. Neither does she relish him hanging around looking thirsty when her friends drop in for their weekly game of kitchen bridge or an afternoon of idle gossip.

And if the husband has a yearning to take up cookery as a retirement hobby that is fine, provided they agree beforehand when the kitchen will be available to him and he takes a course in washing up as well!

Another recipe for domestic disaster is the expanding husband. He has a hobby, perhaps carpentry, or photography, or model railways. Suddenly, he has all the time in the world to indulge in his favourite activity and he needs space for more equipment, for storage. He and his hobby begin to grow and before long can, in the eyes of his wife, reach monster proportions. It is another form of retirement take-over and it can be easily avoided with proper planning.

Such considerations have a bearing on the choice of home in retirement. Will that desirable little bungalow be straining at the seams? Might it not be best to stay put where there are a couple of spare bedrooms that used to be occupied by the children?

12.3   Usefulness

Most people thrive when they feel they are contributing to society rather than being spectators. Using at least some of your leisure time for voluntary work is one way to satisfy that need. It begins to fill some of those gaps: routine, companionship, identity. Status is not important; most of us are happy to leave that behind in the rat race, but identity is important. It is a label that indicates we are still performing some useful function. Mr Jones is no longer 'the Bank Manager' but may well become 'the Teacher' helping to impart reading, writing and simple arithmetic skills in an adult literacy project. Some involvement in the community is perhaps even more important for the single person who is much more likely to feel the loss of companionship that was part of every working day.

You will not have to look far for voluntary work; it has a tendency to find you once it is known that you are available and willing. There is, in fact, a danger that you may take on too much in an initial burst of enthusiasm and find yourself as busy, if not more so, than you were before you took your pension.

Try to be selective. You are now in control and that is the beauty of retirement. The discipline to which you conform is self-discipline. The decisions are yours and you need no longer be a slave to the clock. Set your own pace. You must still have ambitions, targets, dreams even— but isn't it time for a little more of the tortoise mentality and less of the hare?

12.3.1 Voluntary work

The Citizens' Advice Bureau, libraries, churches and hospitals are places to go in search of voluntary work locally. If you have skills and experience that are of particular value, by all means use them; not to do so would be a waste. But change is refreshing and the chance to do something quite different should not be spurned. It is likely to do you as much good as those you are helping.

If you have a favourite charity and would like to help with occasional fund raising, contact them at national level and ask to be put in touch with their local organisation. It doesn't necessarily mean standing on chilly street corners rattling money boxes. A great deal of administration and organisation goes on behind the scenes.

Oxfam, Imperial Cancer Research, Dr Barnardo's, Sue Ryder and other charities have shops in high streets throughout Britain—all of which need volunteers to staff them.

The National Council for Voluntary Organisations, listed at the end of this section, will supply you with information sheets on both paid and unpaid work opportunities. They cost £1, including postage.

The Retired Executive Action Clearing House (REACH) specialises in recruiting and placing retired professional and business people in voluntary organisations with charitable aims. There is no pay for the work but expenses are reimbursed and REACH, itself a charity, charges no fee to individuals or organisations.

Let us examine just a few of the voluntary work openings. If children are close to your heart, the **NSPCC** will gladly tell you how to contact your local group to help with fund raising, but what about the **National Association for the Welfare of Children in Hospital (NAWCH)** or the **National Children's Home (NCH)**?

NAWCH has 70 branches and the voluntary work opportunities vary from visiting children in hospital or in their homes in order to give their mothers some free time, to helping with transport.

NCH runs day care centres, residential children's homes and a telephone care-line. They need volunteers to work alongside professional staff for all of this work and will provide training.

Or perhaps you would like to devote some time to older people? **The Abbeyfield Society** is a federation of voluntary bodies which have set up and maintain houses in which elderly people have their own bedsitting rooms and meals are provided by a resident housekeeper. Volunteers are needed for shopping, gardening, taking residents for day outings and, of course, for helping to expand the work with new schemes.

Maybe you have something to contribute to the community in general. **The Adult Literacy and Basic Skills Unit (ALBSU)** aims to teach basic reading, writing and arithmetic to adults. There is a surprising number who have problems. Even those who can read a little have difficulties with official letters, although you do not have to be illiterate to encounter that phenomenon. ALBSU uses volunteers and will provide training to enable them to teach individuals or help in a group. The head office, listed at the end of the chapter, will supply information about your locality.

The National Association for Mental Health (MIND) has 35,000 helpers at its clubs and day centres, working on social schemes and self-help projects, but volunteers are always needed.

The National Association of Leagues of Hospital Friends will tell you about the nearest league to your neighbourhood. There are more than 1,200 of them helping in hospitals, children's homes, homes of the elderly and hospices. Running hospital shops and tea bars, visiting patients and inmates is all part of their work.

The National Association of Victims Support Schemes provides advice and sympathy to victims of crime and will give training in this work to suitable volunteers. More than 300 training schemes are currently operating.

New Horizons is designed to get people together to work on projects that will benefit their own communities. The charity will provide grants up to £5,000 to existing, or newly formed, groups to help them get their project going. There are conditions: each group must consist of at least ten people and more than half of them must be 60 or over; the project must fill a local need and have a real chance of becoming self-financing. Examples are home repair services for the elderly and cleaning up and maintaining local memorial sites and open spaces.

The Samaritans will train volunteers who man telephones day and night to listen to and speak with people in distress. Your local branch will be in the telephone directory.

Or perhaps you would like to do something for the less fortunate abroad?

Voluntary Service Overseas (VSO) every year sends more than 600 volunteers to work in under-developed communities. They will accept people up to the age of 70, the main qualifications being skill, experience, strong motivation and an adventurous spirit. Bricklayers and business advisers, midwives and mechanics, there is an enormous variety in the skills required. Volunteers serve abroad for two years or more and VSO pays their air fares, medical and other insurance. Accommodation is free and there is payment—at local rates.

The scope is boundless and more organisations and their addresses are given in the end of chapter listing.

12.4 Happiness

Doing something for others gives satisfaction, but this is your retirement and you have every right to do something for yourself after perhaps 40 or more years spent working. All sorts of opportunities that were denied to us when working open up in retirement. Holidays, for instance.

12.4.1   Travel and holidays

You are no longer tied to time. You may travel out of season and stay longer at advantageous prices. An enormous market exists for cheap winter package tours. Hoteliers in southern Spain and other Mediterranean resorts offer low cost accommodation simply to keep their hotels open and their staff employed. Coupled with bargain basement air fares it can cost little more to bask in the sun than it would to stay at home and heat the house.

Attractively priced travel is also available at home. British Rail's Senior Railcard, to which anyone aged 60 or more is entitled, currently costs £16 for one year. The card will obtain you cheap day returns, first and standard class day returns and one day travelcards at half price. They will also cut by one third the cost of savers and supersavers returns, network away-breaks, standard single and open returns and rail rovers. And, if you are taking the grandchildren for a day out, up to four of them under the age of 16 may travel with you in standard class for £1 each.

Discounts may also be had on some ferry services but before making any journey it is wise to check with your local station as there may be some time and route restrictions. To obtain a card, get an application form from the station. You must supply proof of age—passport, birth certificate or your medical card will do.

It does not end there. Possession of the Railcard entitles you, for another £5, to the Rail Europ Senior card. Armed with this you can travel at half price in Belgium, France, Finland, Greece, Luxembourg, the Netherlands, Portugal, Southern Ireland, Spain and in much of Switzerland.

Up to 30 per cent may be saved on railways in Austria, Denmark, Germany, Hungary, Italy, Norway, Sweden and Yugoslavia and on sea crossings by Sealink, Hoverspeed and P&O between Dover and Ostend and Portsmouth and Le Havre when they are part of a rail/sea journey.

Attitudes towards holidays change for most of us in retirement. No longer are they necessary breaks in working routine to enable the batteries to be replenished. The sun-tan status symbol also declines in importance.

Now we have the opportunity to explore at leisure. Change, even from a relaxed routine is, of course, beneficial but many look on holidays in retirement not as a rest but as a stimulant, the chance to seek out unfamiliar places, indulge in different activities and meet new people.

If you need an incentive to explore Britain, why not join **The National Trust**? More than 250 of its historic buildings are open to the public and membership secures you free admission to them. The Trust also protects half a million acres of countryside and miles of coastline.

All of the properties are listed in a handbook issued free to new members. You can join for £21 a year and your partner, or any other member of the family living at the same address, may then join for £12. Life membership is £325 for the over-sixties (£400 for joint membership).

The trust offers a variety of holiday accommodation ranging from basic lodgings for hikers to a beautifully furnished ten-bedroom house in Cornwall. A leaflet of holiday cottages may be obtained for 50p.

But most people do not need help with ideas for holidays. A browse round the local travel agency is normally sufficient. However, some operators specialise in packages for the older generations—mainly long stay winter breaks. **SAGA** predominate in this market.

Activity holidays have grown in popularity because they bring together people with common interests. **H F Holidays, Ltd** is one of the oldest holiday organisations in the country and runs a wide range of special interest holidays from bird watching and bridge to bowls and pony trekking. It began as a Holiday Fellowship primarily for walking holidays and these are still the most popular.

12.4.2   Hobbies and pastimes

Retirement Planning Holiday Courses, under the auspices of the Pre-Retirement Association, provide an introduction to a wide range of hobbies and pastimes at their week-long holidays in Devon. Mornings are devoted to financial planning, pensions, State entitlements, and health; in the afternoons there are sessions for beginners in painting, public speaking, gardening, golf, do-it-yourself, home decorating, car maintenance, photography, flower arranging, bridge, sequence dancing and more.

By the time you reach retirement it is most likely that you will already be adept at one or two, if not more, hobbies and pastimes and may merely wish to devote more time to them. However, a large number do take up new pursuits and change more physically demanding pursuits for new ones of a gentler nature.

Golf and bowls are the favourite sports and it is quite possible to take them up, irrespective of age, and make a reasonable fist of them given a fair degree of physical fitness.

It is not easy to become a golf club member, particularly in the South East where two-year waiting lists are common. You will require sponsorship by existing members. Many clubs offer week-day membership for a start and this is no problem for the retired. It is also less expensive.

There is no membership problem with municipal courses although they are usually crowded and if you are an absolute beginner try yourself out, preferably under the eye of an experienced friend, on a public pitch and putt course. You will discover whether you are ever likely to be able to make contact between club head and ball.

Once a minority recreation, bowls is now a fast developing premier sport. Many local leisure centres have indoor facilities where the learner can get the feel of the game and where woods can be hired.

Swimming is a recommended activity for older people and if you are a non-swimmer, you may find your local pool holds adult beginner classes. Once able to swim the way is open to other sports like sailing, canoeing or angling.

Another popular activity is rambling. There are thousands of miles of public footpaths and bridleways and many have been joined to make continuous trails from 30 to more than 300 miles in length.

The Ramblers' Association is open to membership to retired persons for £6.50. Joint membership costs £8.10. Most of the Association's 320 or so groups organise walks and run social events and the Rambler's Yearbook which comes free with membership contains well over 2,000 bed and breakfast addresses. The price to non-members is £3.50 plus 70p for post and package.

12.5   Thoughtfulness

All of these sports and activities and many more are good for the body, given that you start in good health, but the brain needs exercise as well. Adult education can provide that from Open University degree courses to foreign languages, pottery and painting at night school.

Local authority **Adult Education Institutes** are mainly designed to help older people who wish to take refresher courses or develop special interests. Most classes start in September so get the prospectus from your local Institute, or the public library, in time for enrolment in August.

Apart from learning something useful these courses supply companionship, one of those working life ingredients that can be sorely missed in retirement if you do not do something positive about it. You quickly make friends with others when you are striving together.

The scope of courses is wide. For example, if you are interested in a foreign language there will be classes for beginners, for improvers and for those wishing to take examinations.

Most Institutes offer a very wide range of subjects and if there is a university or polytechnic nearby you can check on whether they run public courses in the evenings or holidays.

The National Institute of Adult Continuing Education publishes *Time to Learn*, a comprehensive list of residential courses, which costs £2.50, including postage.

If you are interested in really serious study there is the **Open University**. Since it was founded in 1969 thousands of retired people have enrolled and every year about 150 of them gain degrees.

You need no academic qualification to enrol. Courses run from February to October and you are expected to work for 12 to 14 hours each week reading texts, watching and listening to broadcasts, carrying out experiments and submitting your work to your tutor. At the end of each successfully completed year you receive a credit; six credits earn a BA degree and eight a BA Honours degree.

You have to apply for enrolment at the latest by Septembr of the preceding year and there may be a waiting list for some courses which can mean a delay of one year.

Not all Open University courses are aimed at a degree. It also runs a leisure series costing between £12.50 and £39.50 for which you receive a study pack, some containing videos. You may enrol at any time.

Numerous organisations offer correspondence courses and the **Council for the Accreditation of Correspondence Colleges** will provide a free list of those it considers bona fide.

For example, there is **The National Extension College** offering a comprehensive range of subjects for GCSE examinations, preparatory courses for the Open University. Leisure courses are varied, ranging from birds and bird watching to successful playwriting. GCSE courses cost from £135 to £165 and leisure subjects from £80.

Short residential courses are provided in many parts of the country by academic establishments, some privately owned.

Earnley Concourse in Chichester runs two, four and seven day courses in arts, crafts, music, drama, dance, literature, food and wine and more which are designed for people with little or no previous knowledge. Costs are from £105 (two days) to £297 (seven days). Some courses incur a supplementary fee. All rooms have private bath and there is a heated swimming pool.

Field Studies Council programmes are held in ten field centres: natural history, ecology and conservation, flowers and plants, birds and animals, landscape and climate, geology, history and architecture are among the subjects. Prices range between around £80 for a week-end for beginners or improvers in water colour techniques at Flatford Mill in Constable country to £360 for two weeks of creative writing at Nettlecombe Court in Somerset.

Workers' Educational Association (WEA) organises talks and demonstrations in most parts of the country. Mostly they are in the form of evening classes but some full-time and part-time courses are available. For details of subjects locally, look up the WEA in your telephone book or contact the national headquarters.

12.6   Still working

It may be that holidays, hobbies and pastimes are not sufficient to keep your brain active. You may feel that you need to have some form of part-time work, indeed financially you may need the additional income. Your State pension will not be jeopardised. Since the abolition of the Earnings Rule in 1989 your pension cannot be eroded if you choose to carry on earning by working after 65 (60 in the case of women). If you have retired from a particular profession eg accountant, bank manager, you may wish to audit the books for various clubs and societies on a chargeable basis.

This can be fine in helping to keep the grey matter in good condition but there are dangers. It is all too easy to cling to the past in order to 'escape' from your retirement. This will not help your partner in coping with this phase in your lives but, of course, it could be helpful to a single person seeking to occupy those many long hours.

Provided the motivation and clear understanding with your partner is correct there should not be a problem but do beware of the trap of missing out on the earlier part of retirement when you are still active and find that you merely pass from a transition of still working straight into older age.

12.7 Conclusion

Retirement: The end of usefulness, the start of decline? No, it is the beginning of a new life. In many ways it can be the most interesting part of your life because you have the time to pursue those things which interest you and give you pleasure while you are still active enough to enjoy them. Interests such as voluntary work may make very little call on your finances yet can be very satisfying.

The choice is yours: the armchair and the television or an active, interesting time spent with your partner and friends. Clearly, planning and forethought about this period in your life will bring its rewards. It is not surprising that those who enjoy it to the full are unanimous in asking, 'How did I ever find time to go to work?'.

Useful addresses

Voluntary work

Abbeyfield Society
186–192 Darkes Lane
Potters Bar
Herts EN6 1AB
(0707 44845)

ALBSU (Adult Literacy and Basic Skills Unit)
Kingsbourne House
229–2312 High Holborn
London WC1V 7DA
(071 405 4017)

Dr Barnardo's
Barkingside
Essex IG6 1QG
(081 550 8822)

Imperial Cancer Research
PO Box 123
44 Lincoln's Inn Fields
London WC2A 3PX
(071 242 0200)

MIND (National Association for Mental Health)
22 Harley Street
London W1N 2ED
(071 637 0741)

National Association of Leagues of Hospital Friends
Fairfax House
Corston Road
Colchester CO1 1RJ
(0206 761 227)

National Association of Victims Support Schemes
Cranmer House
39 Brixton Road
London SW9 6DZ
(071 735 9166)

National Council for Voluntary Organisations
26 Bedford Square
London WC1V 3HU
(071 636 4066)

NAWCH (National Association for the Welfare of Children in Hospital)
Argyle House
Euston Road
London NW1 2SO
(071 833 2041)

NCH (National Children's Home)
85 Highbury Park
London N5 1UD
(071 226 2033)

New Horizons
Paramount House
290–292 Brighton Road
South Croydon CR2 6AG

NSPCC (National Society for the Prevention of Cruelty to Children)
67 Saffron Hill
London EC1N 8RS
(071 242 1626)

Oxfam
274 Banbury Road
Oxford OX2 7DZ
(0865 311 311)

REACH (Retired Executive Action Clearing House)
89 Southwark Street
London SE1 0HD
(071 928 0452)

Sue Ryder Foundation
Sue Ryder House
Cavendish
Suffolk CO10 8AY
(0787 280 252)

The Samaritans
17 Uxbridge Road
Slough SL1 1SN
(0753 32713)

Voluntary Service Overseas
312 Putney Bridge Road
London SW15 2PN
(081 780 2266)

Activity holidays

Earnley Concourse
Earnley
Chichester
Sussex PO20 7JL
(0243 670 392)

Field Studies Council
Preston Montford
Montford Bridge,
Shrewsbury SY4 1HW
(0743 850 674)

H F Holidays, Ltd
Imperial House
Edgware Road
London NW9 5AL
(081 905 9556)

Pre Retirement Planning Holiday Courses
78, Capel Road
East Barnet
Herts EN4 8JF
(081 449 4506)

National Trust (membership and general inquiries)
36 Queen Anne's Gate
London SW1H 9AS
(071 222 9251)

National Trust Enterprises (Holiday cottage leaflet)
PO Box 101
Western Way
Melksham
Wilts SN12 8EA

SAGA Holidays
Bouverie House
Middleburg Square
Folkestone
Kent CT20 1AZ
(0303 47000)

Education

Council for the Accreditation of Correspondence Colleges
27 Marylebone Road
London NW1 5JS
(071 935 5391)

National Extension College
18 Brookmans Avenue
Cambridge CB2 2HN
(0223 316 644)

National Institute of Adult Continuing Education
19b De Montford Street
Leicester LE1 7GE
(0533 551 451)

Open University
PO Box 71
Milton Keynes MK7 6AG
(0908 274 066)

Workers Educational Association
Temple House
9 Upper Berkeley Street
London W1H 8BY
(071 402 5608)

13 Retirement abroad

Despite the potential social pitfalls of moving house, many people dream of retiring abroad. This involves a number of complex matters and you should seek professional advice. This chapter only scratches the surface and helps you ask the right questions.

13.1 Non-residency

The law and practice is covered in some detail in Inland Revenue booklet IR20 *Residents and Non-Residents—Liability to Tax in the United Kingdom*. In this chapter we look at the basic considerations and some specific cases. We must begin by examining the rules which govern residence status as it does not necessarily follow that you will cease to be resident in the UK for tax purposes even though you acquire a home abroad. This is crucially important. If an individual continues to be regarded as UK resident he will generally remain subject to UK tax on his worldwide income. On the other hand, if he is not resident for tax purposes his liability will be confined to UK source income such as rents, UK pensions, dividends from UK companies and interest from UK deposits. Furthermore, a non-resident who is also not ordinarily resident will not normally be subject to CGT (although see 13.4.2—CGT and sales of business).

13.1.1 Residence

The Inland Revenue practice has evolved in a piecemeal way and at present it is largely based upon decided cases. There is relatively little legislation which bears directly on the matter and what little is said raises almost as many questions as it answers. For example, the Taxes Acts clearly contemplate that an individual can be resident in the UK even though he is absent from the country for the entire year!

13.1.2 Available accommodation

At present if you have accommodation available for use in the UK, you are resident here for any year in which you as much as set foot in this country. This is the position even if you do not actually use the accommodation. Moreover, the accommodation may be regarded as available even though you do not own it.

A decided case showed that the availability of a shooting lodge in Scotland was sufficient to make a foreigner resident for years when he came to the UK. The retention of a suite of rooms at a hotel or a club could also render you 'resident' if they were kept in a 'permanent state of readiness' for your use.

There is an exception to this general rule if you are working full time abroad—the exemption does not continue after you have retired.

13.1.3 Does this mean that I will have to sell my property in the UK?

Not necessarily; you could let it, for instance, so that it would not be available for your use although a tax liability would arise on the rents that you received. Or it may be that you can escape by claiming under a double tax treaty. Several of these treaties contain provisions whereby people resident both in the UK and another country may be treated as resident in only one country. But these are exceptions to the general rule that in order to achieve non-resident status you must not have available accommodation.

13.1.4 Visits to the UK

You will be regarded as resident in any tax year in which you spend 183 days or more in this country. Inland Revenue booklet IR20 contains the ominous statement: 'There are no exceptions to this rule', although in practice a dually resident individual may still be able to establish that he should be treated under the provisions of a double tax treaty as if he were not resident. The Revenue at present normally ignores the days of arrival and departure, but there have been cases where even fractions of days have been taken into account, so it would be wise to err on the side of caution.

Even if the 183 days test does not apply, you may still be treated as resident if you make regular visits to the UK which average more than 90 days per tax year, measured over a four year period.

13.1.5 Example: days spent in UK

A has been resident abroad for a number of years, but begins to make visits to the UK. The periods spent in the UK each year are as follows:

1989/90	51 days
1990/91	98 days
1991/92	170 days

If he spends more than 41 days or more in the UK during 1992/93 his visits will have averaged 90 days per annum and he will be regarded as having become resident from 6 April 1992. If he does not visit the UK at all during 1992/93 he will be able to spend 98 days in the UK during 1993/94, as he will then be just within the limit for the period 1990/91–1993/94.

These rules permit some room for manoeuvre in that a continuous period may span two different tax years. It could be, for example, that A spent a single period of 268 days in the UK from 29 December 1990 until 22 September 1991 and still escaped being treated as resident because 98 days fell in the 1990/91 tax year and 170 in 1991/92.

13.1.6   Husband and wife treated separately

Husband and wife are looked at separately as far as residence is concerned. It is quite conceivable therefore that A could be non-resident but have a resident wife and she would then be treated as a separate person for tax purposes, and income tax and CGT would be charged only on her income and gains.

Do bear in mind, however, that if she has accommodation in the UK this will be regarded as available for her husband's use and this could cause him to be treated as resident here.

13.1.7   Ordinary residence

The CGT legislation imposes a liability on individuals who are resident or ordinarily resident for a year of assessment. Ordinary residence corresponds to broadly *habitual* residence so that an individual may remain ordinarily resident for an isolated year when he happens not to be a resident. However, this should not generally be a problem for a person who is retiring abroad as the Inland Revenue will treat a person as not resident or ordinarily resident if he leaves the UK for a period which includes at least three tax years.

13.1.8   Claims under double tax treaties

It is possible for an individual to be simultaneously treated as resident in several countries. A number of double tax treaties contain provisions whereby a dually resident person may be treated as if he were resident in only one country, and set out rules for determining the position. Typically, the tests will be:

(1) If the individual has a permanent home in only one country that is where he will be deemed to be resident.
(2) If the position has not been resolved by (1) then the individual is to be treated as resident where he has the centre of his personal and economic interests.
(3) If the above tests do not resolve the position, the individual is treated as resident where he has an habitual abode.
(4) If he has an habitual abode in both countries, he is deemed to be a resident of the country of which he is a national.

It will be obvious that these tests can be rather uncertain and if you can so arrange matters, it may be that you should seek to resolve the position by ensuring that you do not have a home in the UK. The centre of your personal and economic interests may be in the UK if your family reside here and most of your income and assets are in the UK. Nevertheless, the provisions of certain double tax treaties may be a useful safety net if you find that you have inadvertently made yourself resident in the UK for a particular year. Unfortunately, not all countries have double tax treaties with the UK and some treaties do not contain these provisions. Countries with relevant clauses in the double tax treaties include France, Italy, Portugal, Spain, Switzerland and the United States.

13.1.9 Procedure

Strictly speaking, you are either resident or non-resident for a complete year of assessment. However, in practice, the Revenue treats individuals as not resident and not ordinarily resident for part of a year of assessment. The Revenue summarises its procedure in Booklet IR20 as follows:

'If a person claims he has ceased to be resident and ordinarily resident in the UK, and can produce some evidence for this (for example, that he has sold his house here and set up a permanent home abroad) his claim is usually admitted provisionally with effect from the day following his departure. Normally this provisional ruling is confirmed after he has remained abroad for a period which includes a complete tax year and during which any visits to this country have not amounted to an annual average of three months.

If, however, he cannot produce sufficient evidence, a decision on his claim will be postponed for three years and will then be made by reference to what actually happened in that period. During the three intervening years, his tax liability is computed provisionally on the basis that he remains resident in the UK. He therefore continues to receive the various income tax reliefs due to a resident of the UK except for any tax year in which he does not set foot in the UK. His liability is adjusted, if necessary, when the final decision is made at the end of three years.'

13.2   Domicile

In the longer term, your domicile may be of greater effect than your residence status. Inheritance Tax is charged on certain lifetime transfers and when an estate passes on death. IHT applies to *all* property worldwide if the transferor is domiciled or deemed to be domiciled in the UK (whether or not he is resident here), whereas it applies only to transfers of UK assets if the transferor is domiciled abroad. Similarly, there are income and capital gains tax implications since a foreign domiciled individual who is resident in the UK is not chargeable on overseas income and gains unless they are remitted to this country.

Domicile is a different concept from residence. As we have seen, you can be resident in more than one country but you can only have one domicile. You are domiciled where you regard yourself as 'belonging' or (put another way) the place which is your natural and permanent home. Nationality and residence are relevant factors, but are not conclusive in themselves, and it is quite conceivable that a person may reside in a country for a number of years for personal and/or financial reasons and yet still not be domiciled there. There is a difficult onus of proof which needs to be satisfied before the Revenue and the courts will be satisfied that an original domicile has been abandoned and a new 'domicile of choice' has been acquired.

In practical terms, it will be extremely hard for a person of UK origin who is retiring abroad to establish that he has become domiciled there. If a UK property is retained, the Inland Revnue will generally conclude that the individual had not finally resolved to live the rest of his life abroad, and that he remains legally domiciled in the UK. The retention—or otherwise—of property in the UK is, however, far from being the only factor in this very complex and subtle matter.

Similarly, if such an individual eventually returns to the UK the Inland Revenue may argue that he was domiciled in this country for the whole of his life, notwithstanding that he spends a long period abroad.

If mitigation of IHT is a serious consideration, then it will be advisable to attempt to establish a foreign domicile as soon as possible although in any event as IHT is levied on an individual's worldwide estate if he dies 'deemed domiciled' in the UK, ie within three years of having had UK domicile. The Revenue's domicile questionnaire is shown below (13.11).

Steps to be taken which may help to establish foreign domicile, according to the *Allied Dunbar Tax Guide*, are:

(1)   Develop a long period of residence in the new country.
(2)   Purchase or lease a home there.
(3)   Marry a native of that country.
(4)   Develop business interests there.
(5)   Make arrangements to be buried there.
(6)   Draw up your Will according to the law of the country.
(7)   Exercise political rights in your new country of domicile.
(8)   Arrange to be naturalised (not vital).
(9)   Have your children educated in the new country.
(10)   Close current account in UK and open in new country.
(11)   Resign from all clubs and associations in your former country of domicile and join clubs, etc in your new country.
(12)   Any religious affiliations that you have with your old domicile should be terminated and new ones established in your new domicile.
(13)   Arrange for your family to be with you in your new country.

The above are some of the factors to be considered and the more of these circumstances that can be shown to prevail, the more likely it will be accepted that you have changed your domicile. The Inland Revenue Domicile Questionnaire illustrates how closely the tax authorities scrutinise each case.

13.3   What tax planning steps can be taken in the year of departure?

The most important considerations are usually the timing of retirement, departure abroad and the avoidance of CGT problems on the sale of assets such as a business or shares in a family company.

13.3.1   Golden handshakes

Because of the rules which govern termination payments it will be beneficial in many cases for a person to terminate his employment at the very beginning of a tax year during which he retires abroad. The relief will be maximised if you retire on 6 April and then immediately cease to be resident.

13.3.2   Commutation of pension rights

The decision whether to commute all or part of your pension involves a number of considerations. Expatriates who have a guaranteed income via their company pension are generally able to invest their capital in ways which allow it to grow. At the other extreme, expatriates who have no pension income often end up keeping all their capital on deposit—which is almost certainly the wrong policy in the longer term. The reasons for this difference may be partly emotional but you should not ignore this factor and should, therefore, guard against surrendering all pension entitlement for a cash sum, unless (perhaps) early retirement has been taken.

The tax implications are only one consideration and depend upon the country in which an individual is going to reside. Many countries have double tax treaties which mean that his pension may be taxed only in that country (eg Spain and Portugal) but in other cases there can be a tax advantage in commuting his pension and thus having less income which is taxable in the UK. The expatriate can then invest his lump sum in a way whereby it attracts tax neither in the UK nor in the country of residence. Remember though that often retirement pensions are index-linked and will increase each year in line with inflation; this benefit is lost on commutation.

13.4   Capital gains tax

13.4.1   Sale of main residence

The crucial thing to bear in mind when considering CGT is that it is generally the date on which contracts are exchanged which fixes the date of disposal—not the completion date. So you will not avoid CGT if you exchange contracts whilst you are still resident even though you may have ceased to be resident before you receive payment.

In many cases, it is simply not practical to defer the exchange of contracts until you have left the UK. It may be possible to give your solicitor a power of attorney to act in your absence but this may also produce practical problems.

Fortunately it will often not matter anyway—generally no chargeable gain arises on the disposal of a main residence, but it is necessary to outline the exceptions to that general rule in case they apply in your particular situation. The flow chart below should make the position clear.

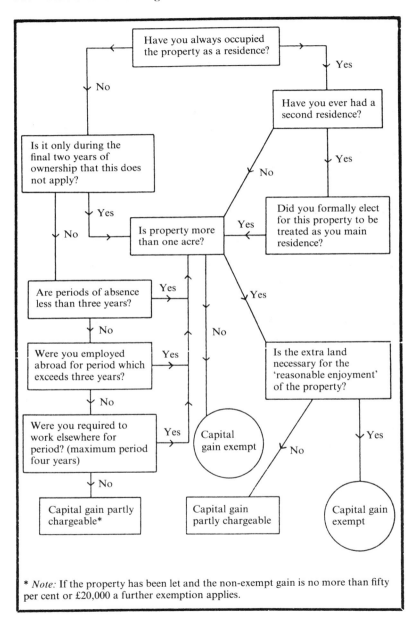

* *Note:* If the property has been let and the non-exempt gain is no more than fifty per cent or £20,000 a further exemption applies.

13.4.2 Sale of a company or business

No CGT will be payable if you dispose of shares in your private company after you have ceased to be resident or ordinarily resident in the UK.

It is more difficult to avoid CGT on the sale of a sole proprietorship or a share in a partnership. By the very nature of things, a purchaser will wish there to be continuity of trading and will not just be acquiring assets which are used in a trade. Indeed, there will often be a significant element of goodwill in the price, and this definitely requires continuity. The problem is that a vendor will not be able to avoid CGT by deferring a sale until he has ceased to be UK resident as CGTA 1979 s12 makes these types of gains subject to CGT if the non-resident has traded in the UK through a branch or agency.

This is a complex area where it is vital that you take professional advice. Remember that for CGT purposes a disposal takes place when you enter into a contract. An oral contract can sometimes count for these purposes so don't leave it too late before you take advice.

13.5 How will your UK income be taxed when you are resident overseas?

As mentioned, liability for income tax on UK income continues even though the recipient is not resident in the UK. Directors' fees from UK resident companies and UK pensions are generally subject to UK tax and withholding tax will be deducted from all but State pension payments. Withholding tax is also deducted at source (at the rate of 25 per cent) from dividends and interest and there may also be a liability to higher rate tax. These liabilities can sometimes be reduced if there is a double tax treaty in force.

13.5.1 Directors' fees and pensions

Directors' fees and remuneration from UK companies will normally remain subject to income tax. Certain double tax treaties provide a possible exemption which covers other types of earned income, for example the relevant part of the UK–USA Treaty states:

Article 14 (Independent personal services). Income derived by an individual who is a resident of the United States from the performance of personal services in an independent capacity may be taxed in the USA. Such income may also be taxed in the UK if (*and only if*):

(a)   the individual is present in the United Kingdom for a period or periods exceeding in the aggregate 183 days in the tax year concerned, or

(b)   the individual has a fixed base regularly available to him in the United Kingdom for the purpose of performing his activities, but only so much thereof as is attributable to services performed in the United Kingdom.

Article 15 (Dependent personal services). Remuneration derived by a resident of the United States in respect of employment exercised in the US shall be taxable only in the USA if:

(a)   the recipient is present in the United Kingdom for a period not exceeding in the aggregate 183 days in the tax year concerned, and

(b)   the remuneration is paid by or on behalf of an employer who is not a resident of the United Kingdom, and

(c)   the remuneration is not borne as such by a permanent establishment or a fixed base which the employer has in the United Kingdom.

The UK–USA Treaty is chosen because it has served as a model as other treaties have been re-negotiated.

Pensions are also normally subject to UK tax, but here again double tax treaties may provide exemption. The UK–USA Treaty stipulates that pensions paid to a resident of the USA shall be taxable only in the USA unless the pension is paid by the UK government or local authority when it may be taxed in the UK. However, UK tax is not charged if the pensioner is a US national as well as resident in the USA. Under normal circumstances, government pensions (eg civil service, armed forces, teachers etc) are always paid after deduction of withholding tax, which is not reclaimable.

13.5.2   Dividends

A non-resident is not normally entitled to the 'tax credit' (ie, tax deducted at source). But, if your investment income is sufficiently large there may be a liability for higher rate tax.

13.5.3   Example: higher rate tax

C receives UK dividends of £30,000 net. If he were resident in the UK he would be entitled to tax credits of 25/75ths, ie £10,000 (these credits can be re-claimed to the extent that the individual is entitled to allowances). However, a non-resident is not normally entitled to claim personal allowances and C may have a higher rate tax liability computed as follows:

Taxable Income	£30,000
Higher Rate Tax Due:	£1,395

The situation may well be different if the individual can claim under a double tax treaty as many of these provide that the recipient can reclaim part of the tax credit and is not subject to higher rate tax. The relief under the treaties generally operates in the following way:

13.5.4   Example: tax relief

C would be entitled to claim the tax credits and to reclaim half of the credit (25%) so that the effective rate of UK withholding tax is 12.5%, ie:

UK dividends	£30,000
Tax credits	10,000
	£40,000
Withholding tax 12½%	5,000

Repayment:

Tax credits	10,000
Less: withholding tax	5,000
Amount due	£5,000

13.5.5   Interest

Untaxed interest is theoretically liable to UK tax but the Inland Revenue does not generally pursue such tax. Extra-Statutory Concession B13 states:

> Where a person not resident in the United Kingdom receives interest (eg bank interest) without deduction of income tax and is not chargeable in the name of an agent under Section 78 of the Taxes Management Act 1970, no action is taken to pursue his liability to income tax except so far as it can be recovered by set-off in a claim to relief (eg for proportionate reliefs and allowances under Section 278 of the Income and Corporation Taxes Act 1988 [previously S.27 ICTA 1970]) in respect of taxed income from United Kingdom sources.

An agent for these purposes is a person who can instruct the bank etc on payments and transfers from the account.

UK residents normally receive bank interest net of tax at the basic rate, but this system does not apply to individuals who are not ordinarily resident. They are able to receive interest gross by signing a certificate confirming to the bank that the beneficial owner of the deposit is not ordinarily resident in the UK.

A number of double tax treaties exempt foreigners from UK tax on interest income, or specify that UK tax shall not exceed a specified rate.

Countries with relevant treaties include: Italy, France, Malta, Portugal, Spain, Switzerland and the United States.

13.5.6 Exempt gilts

Interest paid on certain British government securities is exempt from income tax provided that the beneficial owner is neither resident nor ordinarily resident in the UK. The relevant securities are listed in 13.12. It should be noted that the exemption applies only if the non-resident holds the stock at the date that the interest is paid and does not apply where the non-resident has sold the stock even though the sale may have been 'ex-div'. The Inland Revenue is understood to apply a strict interpretation to the exemption and have denied repayment in such cases.

Application for repayment and for payment of interest without deduction should be made on Forms A1 and A3 obtainable from:

> Inspector of Foreign Dividends
> Lynwood Road
> Thames Ditton
> Surrey
> KT70DP

13.5.7 Rental income

Anybody who rents UK property is required to deduct basic rate tax (25 per cent) from any rents paid to a non-resident landlord and pay the tax to the Revenue. This obligation exists even if the rent is paid into a UK bank account. Moreover, the obligation to deduct basic rate tax applies to the gross amount of the rent, so that if the landlord incurs expenses he is obliged to make a repayment claim. The only way of avoiding these deductions is for the rent to be collected by a UK agent. Rent paid to an agent is paid gross and the agent then becomes liable for assessment. However, the assessment is on the net amount after deducting allowable expenses, so this provides a valuable cash flow benefit.

The following expenses are normally allowable:

(1) Agent's fees
(2) Interest on mortgages and similar loans, but not overdrafts, (the

£30,000 limit does not apply) (subject to the property being let for six months of the year, and being available for letting all year)

(3) An allowance of 10 per cent of the net rents for wear and tear to furniture.

13.5.8 Offshore investment companies

If no relief is due under a double tax treaty, and the investment income is sufficiently large to make the individual subject to higher rate tax, it may make sense to transfer the securities to an offshore investment company. There will then be no UK liability beyond the tax withheld at source. It will generally be sensible to carry out such transfers after you have left the UK as there may otherwise be CGT problems. This is a complex area where professional advice is essential.

13.5.9 Personal allowances

A British subject is entitled to claim personal allowances, which may be set against income subject to UK tax. This entitlement is no longer dependent on the individual's being here for tax purposes.

13.6 What you need to find out about your new country

The above sets out the basics of the UK tax position, but if you are retiring abroad you will need to explore carefully the tax system in the country in which you will reside. It is likely that the basic rules for computing assessable income will be quite different from those which apply in the UK and you will obviously need to take competent local advice.

13.6.1 General strategy—finding out more

Tax legislation changes with bewildering frequency, both in the UK and abroad. Once you have decided to retire abroad you should make enquiries via the Embassy concerned about current rates of tax and allowances. International firms of accountants publish information guides on most developed countries. Beware of the mental trap of assuming that the foreign tax system incorporates the same exemptions as our own. For example, since 1 July 1986 we have had an exemption from CGT for gilts but you may well find that if you settle in (say) Florida that a CGT liability could arise under US tax legislation. Remember that the base cost for foreign CGT purposes may remain your original cost and not the market value when you take up residence abroad. Certain countries such as Canada do compute gains in this way but they are the exception rather than the rule.

13.7   Other financial considerations

The position on UK retirement pensions needs to be carefully explored. After all you have paid in for these benefits for most of your working life! If you have already reached 65 before you retire abroad, there is no problem. You should notify the DSS so that suitable arrangements can be made. You will, however, have your pension frozen unless you reside in an EEC country or one of those countries which has a reciprocal arrangement with the UK in which case you will continue to qualify for annual increases. The DSS issue two helpful booklets, SA29 *Your Social Security and Pension Rights in the European Community* and N138 *Social Security Abroad.*

Even if you have not yet reached the statutory retirement age you will still generally qualify for a National Insurance Retirement Pension in due course, but the amount may be restricted unless you have a full 'contribution record'. There is generally no obligation to pay contributions if you are resident abroad, but it may pay you to make Class 3 voluntary contributions if you are nearing retirement. These will safeguard your right to a full pension and provided you reside in an EEC country, they could be a sensible investment in that the benefits will be 'index linked' and the prospective return can be, therefore, very attractive.

13.7.1   Foreign exchange controls

These vary immensely, but the current position in the UK is relaxed compared to other countries. You may well not foresee any likelihood of wishing to return to the UK or moving to another country, but you might be wise to keep your position as flexible as possible. Preserve your options as far as possible. Find out when you will become subject to exchange controls and investigate what action you could take which could lessen your exposure. Generally it will make sense for the expatriate to import capital/income only as necessary. Again, you should take professional advice.

13.7.2   Inheritance law

Bear in mind that foreign legal systems are quite different from our own. For example, the inheritance laws in Guernsey require a fixed proportion of a deceased person's estate to pass to his children. This kind of rule applies in many continental countries and needs to be borne in mind. Is it what you want to happen? If not, then you need to take legal advice on ways in which you may be able to circumvent these rules, perhaps by making a separate English Will, or creating a settlement.

You should certainly consider making a Will for each jurisdiction in which you have assets.

13.7.3 Purchase of a property overseas

Property, like any investment, has its share of pitfalls. Do remember that the legal situation in any country can change overnight. There are, however, some general rules which apply wherever you are thinking of buying. They may sound obvious, but British people have a tendency to do rash things when in an unfamiliar environment. The combination of glorious sunshine and good local wine can leave the unwary signing things that they would not dream of signing back home.

First and foremost, do *not* try to dispense with the services of a lawyer. On the contrary, sensible people engage one in Britain (usually their own solicitor) and another in the area chosen for their retirement.

Do use a reputable agent, preferably one affiliated to a professional surveying body.

Do not part with any money, however much you are impressed by the developer or the agent, other than through a bank or lawyer. Then at least you will have tangible evidence to support your claim to have purchased the property.

Never buy off a plan, unless a large section of the development is already completed. If you must do so, however, insist on a bank or insurance company guarantee of completion. Check the development's water and electricity sources.

The choice of property is so wide and the pressure of the sales pitch so enticing that you must be well prepared before you negotiate.

Prepare a checklist and make the agent or vendor complete a copy. You should get a majority of ticks and the negatives will help you to reduce the price if it has been pitched artificially high. Even the price of a new property is subject to negotiation, no matter what the brochure says.

You will want to know the details that will have a direct bearing on the lifestyle you wish to enjoy. Particularly if you are looking at an apartment.

- Is the development predominantly English occupied or multi-national?
- Can I meet one or two of the occupants?
- Is membership of any clubs included: eg beach, riding, golf, country, tennis, bowls?
- If not, are there any centres for these sports close by and are there any special concessions on membership fees?
- Is there a heated swimming pool?
- Is a garage included?
- Is there a club room and bar?
- Is there a clinic with an English speaking doctor in the complex?
- Is there a telephone included or a telephone point?
- Is there a bus service to the nearest town?
- Is there a taxi point and what is the fare to the nearest town/airport?
- What security arrangements exist? 24 hour patrol? Telephone linked to a central point?
- Is there a television point?
- Does it include a mooring?
- Is a safe or any furniture included in the price?
- Can somebody build in front of the beautiful view?
- Will the developer maintain an office on the site?
- What are the charges for the upkeep of communal gardens, swimming pool and outside painting, etc? How often are they revised?
- Where is the nearest shopping complex and does it contain a pharmacy?
- Is the apartment air-conditioned?
- Does it include any of the following equipment: dishwasher, washing machine, refrigerator, waste disposal unit and bathroom heater?

Some developments will offer most of these benefits and many will be able to score 14 or above. Your own priorities will determine whether this will be sufficient to warrant a purchase.

Having decided that you like the area and that the property is also to ` your liking, we suggest *most strongly* that you pay careful attention to the following list:

(1)   Engage a lawyer—preferably one who is bi-lingual and who understands the property laws in the country where you wish to live.
(2)   Do not be tempted by the deals which appear to save you money—usually they don't in the long run.
(3)   Check the credentials of the agent and the developer.
(4)   Make sure that the vendor has full and proper title to the property he is setting out to sell you.
(5)   See the property 'in the flesh'—and try to see it 'warts and all', not merely in bright warm sunshine and mild spring breezes. If you're going to live there, you should see it in the winter time.
(6)   Do not over commit yourself financially.
(7)   Make any transfers of money formally, preferably by notarised document, through your own bank and/or lawyer.
(8)   Make sure you are happy to live—all the year round—in the community and area of which your intending property is part.

Finally, do take care and don't sign *anything* until you have sought professional advice. A number of people have lost money in property deals abroad, particularly in Spain, and not just at the hands of foreign companies.

The next section deals with two classes of people who come to the UK from abroad, and addresses the questions:

- What action should UK expatriates take before returning home?
- How should foreigners arrange their affairs if they retire to the UK?

13.8   UK expatriates returning home

Expatriates who return to the UK do not generally qualify for any income tax or CGT concessions. They become liable to UK tax on their worldwide income and gains once they become resident and ordinarily resident in the UK. Tax planning in these situations consists mainly in timing the date of return, and ensuring that certain pitfalls are avoided.

The tax position can be very complicated and you would be well advised to take professional advice from an accountant, solicitor etc. You may also find the *Allied Dunbar Expatriate Tax and Investment Guide* of value. However, the following checklist may be of assistance in putting you on the right lines.

13.8.1   Checklist for expatriates about to return to the UK

(1)   Should capital gains be realised before you resume residence in the UK and become subject to CGT? Will there be a sale of a UK property and, if so, will it be covered by the main residence exemption?

(2)   Should capital gains be realised before the start of the tax year in which you return to the UK? (This will normally be advisable if you have been non-resident for less than 36 months.)

(3)   Should UK bank deposit accounts be closed before the start of the tax year in which you return to the UK to avoid UK tax liability on interest? However, consider possible liability for foreign tax.

(4)   Consider a way of 'bringing forward' income on foreign securities etc, eg by selling stocks cum-div and repurchasing ex-div. Should foreign bank deposit accounts be closed immediately before you return to the UK? Again you should bear in mind the possible tax implications in the foreign country in which you are resident.

(5)   Ensure that pay for any terminal leave period will not attract UK tax.

(6)   There may be cases where liability for VAT can be avoided by arranging for professional advisers to invoice you while you are non-resident.

13.9   Golden handshakes

Finally, it is worth mentioning in this context that a special relief may be available for expatriates who return to the UK and receive a golden handshake after their return.

A termination payment is completely exempt where foreign service represents 75 per cent of the total period of employment or (where the employment lasted more than 20 years) at least 50 per cent of the period was spent in foreign service during the last 20 years. The definition of foreign service is that the employee was either not resident or not ordinarily resident or entitled to the 100 per cent deduction as having met the 365 day test.

13.9.1   Example: Foreign service

A was non-resident in the UK from 1972–1984. He then qualified for the 100% deduction from 1984 until 1986, so that he was not subject to UK tax on his salary even though he was resident. He then worked in the UK. In 1992 he retired and received compensation of £80,000. He had spent 16 years working abroad and 4 years working in the UK $\frac{16\text{ years}}{20\text{ years}} = 80\%$ and so the compensation of £80,000 is exempt.

Where the above conditions are not satisfied the employee is entitled to an extension to the £30,000 exemption available to UK residents generally which is determined by the formula:

$$\frac{\text{Foreign service}}{\text{Total period of employment}}$$

This fraction is applied to the amount of the golden handshake after deduction of the £30,000 exemption.

13.9.2 Example: extension of £30,000 exemption

Suppose A's employment had started in 1977. The fraction

$$\frac{\text{Foreign service (10 years)}}{\text{Total period of employment (14 years)}}$$

then becomes 71 per cent, so the compensation is not completely exempt. The taxable amount would be arrived at as follows:

Compensation	£80,000
Less: 'normal exemption'	£30,000
	£50,000
10/14ths thereof	£35,714
Taxable amount	£14,286

If A had other taxble income of £28,000 (after allowances but including his salary from the job) the tax payable on the £14,286 would be computed as follows:

Total taxable income £42,286 tax thereon	£11,353.40
Deduct tax payable on £28,000	5,746.25
	5,607.15

Income tax actually payable on the £80,000 compensation is £5,607.15

13.10   Retiring to the UK—a tax haven!

The UK can be a tax haven for persons of foreign domicile who settle here but who do not become domiciled here. At present if you are not domiciled in the UK and have overseas income and capital gains, you need not pay tax unless and until you remit them here, so payment of UK tax on overseas income and gains becomes a *voluntary* activity, provided that you can arrange your affairs in the right way!

We have already discussed the concept of domicile (see 13.2) and it will be apparent that you may reside in the UK for a number of years and still not be domiciled here. A special rule applies for IHT purposes whereby you will be deemed to be domiciled in the UK if you have been resident for 17 of the preceding 20 tax years, but this rule does not affect the favourable treatment for income tax and CGT purposes.

13.10.1   Avoiding liability on money that you bring into the UK

The most important steps to take from a practical point of view are the establishment of several different offshore bank accounts so that capital and accumulated income can be clearly identified. The point is that if you make remittances to the UK from a 'mixed' account which contains both capital and accumulated income, the Inland Revenue will argue that the remittances are to be identified primarily with income: ie the worst possible basis! However, this potential problem is easily overcome by opening separate offshore bank accounts.

Basically, the balance on your account at the date you come to the UK to take up residence is regarded as capital. In future, overseas income should be credited to a separate account, and this includes interest on your existing overseas bank account. Furthermore, a third account needs to be opened to receive the proceeds of sales of overseas securities and other foreign assets which show capital gains. Other sale proceeds should be credited to your main capital account.

Obviously, your strategy should be to live off your capital account, and to supplement this (if necessary) by remittances from the account which contains capital gains. Only as a last resort should you make remittances from the income account if they take your taxable income over the personal allowance. In this way you will legitimately have minimal overseas income and gains to declare.

Furthermore, there are a number of ways in which you can use the balance on your overseas income account without incurring a UK tax liability. Firstly, you can spend the money outside the UK (for example on holidays) or you can invest it (but be careful of the way in which you deal with the position when you sell the investment or you may end up remitting income without meaning to do so). In an emergency you may be able to rely on court decisions which indicate that a husband who gives his wife accumulated overseas income is not liable to income tax when she remits it, as it is capital in her hands! However, you should take professional advice before doing this in view of the recent trend of House of Lords' decisions.

Another point worth bearing in mind, but one that needs careful handling, is that if you have just one overseas investment and you sell it, it is arguable that accumulated income from this particular source may be safely remitted in the following tax year. It would be sensible to discuss this with your accountant or professional adviser first, but it can be a way of remitting money to the UK without incurring an income tax liability.

A foreign domiciled person is still liable to tax in the normal way on income and gains arising in the UK, so you should avoid UK investments. If you wish to invest in the UK Stock Market the best way is to do so via an offshore fund in the Isle of Man or Channel Islands and many unit trust and investment groups have funds which meet this requirement.

An individual can realise chargeable capital gains up to a certain level each year without any CGT liability because they are covered by the annual exemption. Therefore, if you have no UK capital gains you can remit an appropriate part of the capital gains account without a tax liability.

13.10.2 Inheritance tax planning

Until the 17 year rule bites you will not be subject to UK IHT on capital transfers of foreign assets. Foreign assets include money held in overseas bank accounts, shares in foreign companies and bearer securities actually held overseas. It may well be wise to hold UK property through a foreign investment company as the shares in such a company are 'excluded property' (ie not subject to IHT when owned by a person of foreign domicile), and this effectively converts UK assets into foreign property. As the 17 year deadline approaches, it may also be appropriate to make a settlement of overseas assets as this will take them outside the ambit of IHT even though you may subsequently be deemed to have UK domicile. Substantial savings of IHT are possible by taking steps of this nature, but it is essential to take competent professional advice.

13.11   INLAND REVENUE DOMICILE QUESTIONNAIRE

Name: ....   Reference: ....

The following information is requested in order that the claim to be not domiciled in the United Kingdom may be given consideration.

1   Where and when were you born?   _____

2   In what country was your father domiciled
    at the date of your birth? (in the case of a
    country with a Federal system, the particu-
    lar State, Province, etc. should be stated.)   _____

3   What changes, if any, took place in your
    father's domicile during your minority?   _____

4   If your father is dead, state his full name and
    the date and place of his death.   _____

5   In what country do you consider that you
    are domiciled and on what grounds? (in the
    case of a country with a Federal system, the
    particular State, Province, etc should be
    stated.)   _____

6   Whether any accommodation is retained
    for your use in that territory and, if so, the
    address, the nature of the accommodation
    and whether it is kept in a permanent state
    of readiness for your occupation.   _____

7   What are your business, personal, social or
    other connections with that territory?   _____

8   If you are married, where do your spouse
    and any children reside?   _____

9   Is any accommodation retained for your use
    in the United Kingdom and, if so, the
    address and nature of the accommodation?   _____

10 What periods have you spent in the United
    Kingdom during each of the past 10 years?   _____

11 The reason for your residence in the United
    Kingdom, eg whether in connection with
    business or employment (in which event,
    details of the business or employment and
    the nature of the position held should be
    stated), or the education of children.   _____

12 What are your intentions for the future; and
    if not to stay permanently in the United
    Kingdom, the circumstances in which it is
    envisaged that residence will cease?   _____

Date: ....   Signature: ....
                                             Address: ....
                                                        ....
                                                        ....

13.12 Gilts exempt from tax for non-UK residents:

$2\frac{1}{2}\%$	Treasury 2004
$3\frac{1}{2}\%$	War Loan 1952 or after
$5\frac{1}{2}\%$	Treasury 2008–12
$5\frac{3}{4}\%$	Funding 1987–91
6%	Funding 1993
$6\frac{3}{4}\%$	Treasury 1995–98
$7\frac{3}{4}\%$	Treasury 2012–15
8%	Treasury 1992
8%	Treasury 2002–6
$8\frac{1}{4}\%$	Treasury 1987–90
$8\frac{1}{2}\%$	Treasury 2000
$8\frac{1}{2}\%$	Treasury 2007
$8\frac{3}{4}\%$	Treasury 1997
9%	Treasury 1994
9%	Treasury 1992–96
9%	Conversion 2000
9%	Treasury 2008
$9\frac{1}{2}\%$	Treasury 1999
10%	Treasury (CV) 1991
10%	Treasury 1993
10%	Treasury 1994
$10\frac{1}{2}\%$	Treasury (CV) 1992
11%	Exchequer 1990
$12\frac{1}{2}\%$	Treasury 1993
$12\frac{3}{4}\%$	Treasury 1992
$12\frac{3}{4}\%$	Treasury 1995
13%	Treasury 1990
$13\frac{1}{4}\%$	Exchequer 1996
$13\frac{1}{4}\%$	Treasury 1997
$13\frac{3}{4}\%$	Treasury 1993
$14\frac{1}{2}\%$	Treasury 1994
$15\frac{1}{4}\%$	Treasury 1996
$15\frac{1}{2}\%$	Treasury 1998

14   Health matters

Successful retirement provides an opportunity to spend the last third of your life without too much financial or domestic responsibility, to do the things you enjoy doing and hopefully continuing to make a contribution to the community.

Over many years of retirement counselling, money and health were cited as the main sources of anxiety at pre-retirement discussions. Now, however, probably because of better occupational pensions, removal of the earnings rule in retirement and a wider range of opportunities for part-time work, a possible fall in income seems to present less of a worry. And here it is worth noting that, at the outset, financial thought tends to centre on the fall in income and neglect the considerably reduced expenditure on items such as pensions, mortgage, National Insurance contributions, clothes, travel to work, etc. In practice, spending money turns out to be more than was originally expected.

Thus health now often represents a main source of anxiety, and sensibly so, because with poor health or major disability, enjoyment is difficult.

14.1   Understanding the problem

Three main, possibly quite surprising, factors determine health in retirement. The first is obviously the mental and physical state you take into retirement. If you have lived prudently and invested wisely in health and have inherited good long-living genes, your health should continue to be good. And, in any case, having got so far without mishap, you can consider yourself a survivor.

Second, and this could be the surprising point, it is important to accept that health is not just the absence of disease, it is a positive entity reflecting general well-being, resulting from good physical, mental and social adjustment. It means being in tune with your emotional and physical environment.

Third comes the understanding of simple health rules which minimise the inevitable effects of aging. Aging is not a disease but a series of changes brought on largely by the wear and tear of life, often unrelated to calendar age but inevitably related to how one has lived previously. Wise people take care not to wear themselves out prematurely. Workaholics have little steam left in the retirement boilers and may last less long.

Against this background it should be clear that the maintenance of well-being is the critical and probably most controllable factor in staying well. As it is a reflection of life in general which has up to now been work centred, it is essential to understand the changes to which you have to adjust, both personally and in your relationships when you retire. Obviously, if you've hated or been bored stiff by your work, you can't wait to retire and will have few problems. But for many of us, the sudden loss of work and the motivation it provides, produces a vacuum which may be difficult to fill, particularly if associated with resentment at, as it were, being seemingly thrown on the scrap-heap.

There thus has to be an action plan to maintain well-being and health in retirement. This starts by realising that work, apart from providing money, gives status, identity and association with the work group. The loss of these can, unless well handled, amount to bereavement with similar deprivations.

The trick, then, of retiring successfully hinges round establishing a new status and identity and motivation. The 25–30 years life expectancy you still have is far too long a time to drift about doing nothing in particular. There have to be commitments to fill the day and get you to bed tired enough to sleep.

Retirement planning thus starts with the realisation that there is, or may be, a problem. New opportunities and challenges present themselves. As with the other main phases of life, appropriate plans have to be made and options examined. Successful retirement seldom 'just happens'.

The attributes of work have to be replaced by a new series of well-motivated and day-filling activities to provide a new and meaningful identity. But as well as this, it is sensible to think through the problems of the next 20 or so years, like making or revising a Will and beginning to plan for possible frailty, or how best to cope when there's only one of you.

Retirement can be summarised in two ways. First a quote from the American comedian W C Fields who, when asked about retirement, said 'if I'd known I was going to live so long I would have taken more care of myself'. And secondly, and perhaps more meaningfully, the successful retired person is the one who, a year after retirement, wonders how he ever had time to go to work and is purposefully engaged and busy. There are several main areas of concern.

14.1.1 Time planning

What are you going to do? Do you want full or part-time work? Voluntary or paid? Particularly if retirement is early, there is a lot to be said for having a formal job or appointment. It is motivational and brings you into contact with other people. There needs to be something in the diary for tomorrow.

Important, too, is to think about how much time you and your partner want to spend together and how much separately. Getting under each other's feet is very much a hazard of retirement and if you have been together all day it's not surprising that there's nothing to talk about over supper.

In these days of earlier formal retirement, a third career, not necessarily fully salaried, is a real possibility (see chapter 11). But whatever the choices, there is plenty of advice around about things to do and who needs help.

14.1.2 Where to do it

Moving to a better climate or situation may be tempting but beware: you need all the contacts you have and becoming a newcomer in a strange place can be very lonely. There may be a need for a different house, larger or smaller, garden or no garden, stairs or lift to a flat, etc, in the same area. Houses, especially after the children have grown up, are an under-used asset. In retirement they are lived in, can be untidy and it is wise to plan for each of you to have your own 'nag proof' territory where your own interests can be pursued without friction. This may mean a larger rather than a smaller house but territory is precious even if it's only a shed in the garden for dad.

If change is contemplated, give thought to later on. Frailty, arthritis, granny flats, etc.

14.2   Financial planning

This book is largely about financial planning. The section on health is to help you make it worthwhile and possibly to enjoy your pension but there are some points related to well-being that are also related to finance and hence worth mention in this section.

First, retirement is about enjoyment without anxiety. Now is the time with expert and ongoing advice, to make your money work for you. Spend it on the priorities you have identified and activities you've considered under time planning. For instance, there may be no necessity to leave money to your children. If asked, they would mostly prefer you to be happy and solvent yourselves.

Second, as well-being in later life hinges round reducing anxiety, financial planning should be done jointly and together. There will one day be only one of you, probably the woman, and she needs to know how she will stand financially and that proper Wills etc have been made. This is covered in chapter 9, but it is surprising how many wives worry because they don't know if there is a Will, what is in it, and so on.

Third is to accept that making the most of financial reserves is a technical activity which needs expert and flexible advice. Not only does the law change about taxation and so on but also your priorities change as you get older so that regular revision is sensible.

14.3   Relationships and anxiety

As I've said, the main factor in maintaining well-being is to minimise sources of friction and anxiety. This requires the maturity to discuss problems rather than to bury them. With no workplace to go to, one is thrown back on family and other social relationships and these may need repair and fostering. Also attitudes and roles change. A man retiring can now do more of the domestic chores, he might even go on a cooking course. Houses are more fully used and there are more opportunities to do things together. All this requires discussion as, I suggest, do attitudes to serious illness. We all fear these disabling ills and tend to push the problems to the back of our minds. But there is a case for discussing, well in advance, what you want to do, eg who is told what about serious illness and to consider having an enduring power of attorney (see 9.5). Such plans can always be altered but they do provide, if known to the family, a comforting fall-back position.

14.4   Single people

So far, the outlines given for fostering well-being refer to partnerships of several possible sorts but from what I have said, the promotion of well-being hinges round activities and relationships. A single person, of either sex, who may be a workaholic and inherently bad at relationships, will probably be much more vulnerable in retirement. In choosing where to live and what to do such people have to give much more thought to avoiding isolation by what they do and possibly where they live. Obviously, of course, a good supportive family makes this very much easier.

Widows and widowers have similar but more acute problems of adjustment and may be considerably helped by specialist counselling agencies like CRUSE. Similarly, most good retirement counselling courses include sessions for single people. Loneliness is the main problem of getting older.

Useful addresses

Age Concern England
Bernard Sunley House
60 Pitcairn Road
Mitcham
Surrey
CR4 3LL
Tel: 071–640 5431

Alzheimer's Disease Society
158–160 Balham High Road
London
SW12 9BN
Tel: 071–675 6557/8/9/0

Arthritis and Rheumatism Council (ARC)
41 Eagle Street
London
WC1R 4AR
Tel: 071–405 8572

BACUP (British Association of Cancer United Patients)
121–123 Charterhouse Street
London
EC1M 6AA
Tel: 071–608 1661
Freeline: 0800–181199

Chest, Heart and Stroke Association
Tavistock House North
Tavistock Square
London
WC1H 9JE
Tel: 071–387 3012

CRUSE
126 Sheen Road
Richmond
Surrey
Tel: 081–940 4818

Hospice Information Service
St Christopher's Hospice
51–59 Lawrie Park Road
Sydenham
London
SE26 6DZ
Tel: 071–778 9252

Parkinson's Disease Society of the UK Ltd
36 Portland Place
London
W1N 3DG
Tel: 071-255 2432

REACH (Retired Executives Action (Clearing-House))
89 Southwark Street
London
SE1 0HD
Tel: 071–928 0452

Relate: National Marriage Guidance
Herbert Gray College
Little Church Street
Rugby
Warwickshire
CV21 3AP
Tel: 0788–73241

15 Physical health and fitness

There are two disciplines to maintaining vitality in retirement and these are the disciplines of regular mental and physical activity. All living organisms become inert if they are not fully exercised and challenged by their environment. The body exists to be used judiciously. Thus a major contribution to growing old gracefully and appearing younger than you might be, is the essential stretching of bones and joints and muscles—and the brain. It may surprise you to know that just as exercise maintains muscle strength, the brain needs regular 'work' to keep it on the ball and responsive, otherwise it gets lazy.

With these necessities in mind, we will now examine in a little more detail the main needs and problems of the physical and mental body systems in relation to aging.

15.1 Bones, joints and strength

Although skeletons in museums look strong and static like the scaffolding or girders of a building, bone is in fact a living substance which responds to stress and usage. Thus a major problem for astronauts during prolonged weightlessness is loss of bone calcium because the bones are not then load carrying. In ordinary life, particularly for men, this is not often a serious problem. Because, however, of hormone changes at the menopause, women begin to lose calcium and there may be a risk of easy fractures of hip, wrist and spine from a trivial fall. Fractures in older women are in fact a major economic and medical problem and a great deal of research is currently being done on early detection of the vulnerable and prevention of calcium loss.

At the present time, early 1991, the best way for a woman of minimising the risk of brittle bones, is regular physical exercise before and after the menopause. It may well be, that, in the near future, other treatments such as hormone replacement therapy will become advisable but this is still experimental.

Joints in older people over, say, 65 can be regarded as similar to garden gates and cupboard doors. If you only half open your garden gate when you go out, it will creak, but not if you open it fully. The same is true of aging joints. To minimise creaking and maintain suppleness they need regular bending and stretching by exercises to put them through their full range of movements. You can invent these for yourself, or visit almost any book store, or read women's magazines, in which exercise schedules abound.

'Aerobic' is today's catch word for exercise. All, in grammatical fact, it implies, is getting out of breath. Any physical activity that does this is respectably aerobic and keeps you in with Jane Fonda and her ilk.

Heart muscle responds in the same way as main body muscle. It needs a regular workload to keep it strong. Getting mildly out of breath makes the heart beat faster and work better.

Half an hour of this exercise most days, all through the year, is required. This can be in any way you either positively enjoy or are least bored by. Walking, jogging, dancing, swimming, games, etc. Gardening is good because it involves bending and stretching. Swimming may not be everyone's cup of chlorine but it uses all the muscle groups and is exercise without weight bearing. A static bicycle takes up little room, is weather-proof and also enjoyed by grandchildren, but even going up and down stairs briskly often enough, stresses most of the right bits and gets you out of breath. If you keep reasonably physically active, you could get a decent size dog to take out. You will feel better, sleep better and function more efficiently. Older people often claim difficulty in sleeping. A main requisite of sleep is to be tired which doesn't result from doing nothing much all day.

15.2 Keeping warm

Because it's inevitable that older people are more sensitive to cold, there is nothing to be gained by exhibiting foolhardy pride in not wrapping up well in cold weather. A lot of heat, for instance, is lost via the head and neck, so warm, perhaps woolly, hats and scarves are sensible. If you drive a lot in winter, keep extra warm things in the boot in case of a breakdown.

With advancing age, over 60, skin insulation breaks down, causing wrinkling and the blood supply diminishes, in effect the central heating system is aging. Thus you can expect to need more heat in the house and thicker clothes outside. Taking your regular exercise in winter wrap up well and don't despise warm underclothes.

In dealing with aging, it is axiomatic that it is easier to retain what you have than to regain what is lost. Very true of both warmth and strength.

My old gardener, who recently retired at the age of 83 could, until his last six months, still do a full day's physical work, because this is what he'd always done.

15.3   Vision

As the lens in the eye loses its elasticity with age, its focusing power diminishes and the near point of the normal eye retreats until the arms are not long enough and the print too small for focusing. Most people require reading glasses from middle age onwards. These are simply convex lenses to bring the near point back within reach. This is a normal age change.

A similar change happens to short sighted people, as their near point is too close they may, with luck, finish up with it more or less in the right place and manage to do without glasses.

Astigmatism, due to irregularity of the surface of the eye, remains unchanged with age.

The important feature of the older eye is that it requires more light. We tend to be mean about light in the home, so be sure to have a decent light to work with and read by and adequate lighting on stairs, corridors and above all, in the kitchen.

If you do fine work at a distance different from reading, it's worth getting a special pair of glasses for this precise focal distance. They are not expensive.

All spot checks of drivers' vision show a high proportion have visual defects that could and should be remedied by eye testing and different glasses. Eye strain is a bit of a myth but go on getting your eyes tested even if it costs a little money. Also, it's more comfortable to control glare with sunglasses, particularly on holiday, but do go for neutral colours.

Two common eye diseases in later life are cataract and glaucoma. The latter runs in families and is due to raised pressure within the eye, from blockage of the drainage system which runs round the edges of the pupil. It can be acute or chronic and if acute can cause blindness. Sudden pain, severe headaches over the eye and possibly vomiting, should be taken straight to the doctor or eye centre to preserve vision. Acute glaucoma is a real emergency, an operation to re-establish drainage may be needed or eye drops to dilate the pupil may improve it.

There's a simple screening test to measure the pressure in the eye and identify people who, with raised pressure, may be vulnerable to glaucoma which is carried out at many screening centres. Glaucoma is familial so that if you have a family history your 'eye pressure' should be checked regularly.

Cataract is due to increasing opacity of the lens and may often be related to diabetes. Relatively simple operations for lens replacement by a plastic insert are now available and very satisfactory.

15.4   Hearing

Hearing also deteriorates with age but because it's less critical than vision, one can get by with some loss of hearing without too much difficulty but deafness does isolate and tends to induce paranoia. Now that hearing aids are smaller and more sophisticated they are, at long last, becoming more socially acceptable.

You can get your hearing tested in the NHS and it's useful to have a base line. Not all forms of deafness, as when the actual nerve is damaged, can be helped by a hearing aid but certainly, if you have a hearing problem, it's worth trying an aid.

But beware, they are expensive and heavily sold. Don't part with your money until several day's use has convinced you of the benefit. Also make sure if, for instance your fingers are arthritic, that you can manage the controls. My 90 year old mother didn't use hers very much because I finally discovered that the switch and the battery change were too fiddly for her fingers. Old fashioned aids may be easier to manage and are still available.

There are two parts to hearing, the reception and the speech. We all know how difficult it is for the driver to make out what the back seat person is on about. If there is a deaf family person, much help can be given by speaking, not shouting, clearly, slowly and at them. Given the topic in context one can make up a lot of the detail.

Surgery now has much more to offer in terms of repair and replacement for certain ear diseases so if you have a problem go to your doctor and ask to see a specialist.

The ear in fact has two main functions, hearing and balance, so that some ear diseases cause giddiness and vice versa. Menière's disease is the commonest and usually responds to treatment. It is thought to be largely due to raised pressure in the balancing organs but certainly it causes considerable and disabling giddiness for short periods.

The commonest and most infuriating upset and it is age related, is tinnitus—noises in the ear, rushing, whistling, humming, continuous, intermittent, loud and soft and so on. Tinnitus sometimes has an identifiable cause which may be treatable and all cases should certainly be investigated. But mostly it's a mystery and if severe can drive one nearly crazy. Usually little can be done directly to reduce it but there are tricks like masking sound to make hearing possible. As a last resort, in the worst cases, it may be necessary to destroy the nerve but this causes deafness. But any case of tinnitus should be investigated by an expert and there is a very helpful Tinnitus Society which gives advice. Also, the Royal Society for the Deaf can give a wide range of useful advice on all hearing-related matters.

15.5 Diet and digestion

A main reason for the biological supremacy of homo sapiens is the flexibility of its digestive system. If we couldn't live satisfactorily—as indeed we do—on such a wide range of foods, most of the currently publicised diets would be lethal. In my view, more nonsense is talked and more doubt engendered by the discussion of diet than any other medically related topic.

Outside badly run institutions there is little significant malnutrition in the United Kingdom. In fact, over-nutrition—obesity—is the commonest disease involving about 30% of the population who are overweight, because, on the whole, thin people live longer than fat ones.

As eating is very much a matter of habit, ie we enjoy what we're used to eating and tend to resent change, it is obviously important to give children sensible dietary habits. Diseases like coronary thrombosis are diet related but when it comes to retirement we are mostly survivors, perhaps in spite of our past diets. So in my view we need not worry too much about diet except under two sets of circumstances. First if we have an established diet related problem like diabetes, an allergy or being in a high risk coronary category. Second is to keep our weight within reasonable (10% of ideal) limits. Remember here that exercise is vital: the less there is of you to cart around the easier it is to do!

In assessing your dietetic behaviour, or before you start worrying, it's sensible to define the odds, ie get a simple health check. If your cholesterol levels are normal, enjoy strawberries and cream; if not, stick to unsaturated vegetable fats.

It is sensible, in thinking about eating, to make the distinction between nutrition and diet. The former are the items in the diet, like vitamins, minerals, etc, required by the body as building bricks. The latter is the totality of what we eat, determined by culture, geography and habit. Primary foodstuffs like fats, carbohydrates and proteins are to a considerable degree interchangeable by the digestive system.

A normally functioning digestive system is marvellously flexible. It takes in what is delivered through the mouth, breaks the food down into its constituent chemical substances, absorbs what it can or wants and gets rid of the residue as urine or faeces. It is rather like dismantling a lego construction and using the bits to make something quite different.

Against this background the rules of diet for older people with good digestions is simple.

(1)   Go on enjoying your meals and experiment with new dishes now you have time.

(2)   Control your weight: obesity is very largely due to a credit account of eating too many calories.

(3)   Make sure your diet contains plenty of fresh food—fruit and vegetables—but the virtues of so-called health and organic foods are reflected more in additional price than in additional value, ie they're largely a racket. There is no proven evidence that their additional value matches the price.

(4)   It is sensible over life to cut down on amount of fats as they do contribute to coronary heart disease.

(5) The digestive system works on a squeeze-through basis, it gets less efficient with age so needs more bulk to work on, ie lots of fibre. A high fibre diet also has other virtues but All-Bran certainly makes the bowels go round.

(6) Be careful, especially in warm weather, to keep up fluid intake. Older people tend to cut down on fluids towards the end of the day in the hope that this will stop them getting up at night. It won't because the kidneys work differently. Anything you drink counts as fluid, alcohol is high calorie and adds to weight. Modest drinkers live longer than teetotallers so enjoy 'a drink' if this is what you like.

(7) Cut down on salt. There is a relationship between salt and high blood pressure and we're used to far more salt than we need—a matter of habit.

For most of us in later life eating is a major pleasure to be legitimately indulged, keeping an eye on the waist line. There are plenty of more important things to worry about like being bored and lonely.

15.6 Attitudes to illness

It usually surprises people to be told that, particularly in terms of early diagnosis, they are initially more important than the doctor. It is, in fact, trite but true to point out that symptoms do not become 'official' until they are taken to the doctor. The individual decides if and when to seek help for their dis-ease. In basic terms you usually decide whether to go to work or to the doctor. Usually of course, with acute disease, the choice is obvious but for a wide range of other disabilities and anxieties there is both a choice and a host of possible reasons for not going.

15.7 Cancer

Most of us as we get older are lucky if every now and again we don't begin to think that the mildest of symptoms may be cancer and are afraid of them. Because of this fear, we put off going to the surgery hoping that the pain or lump or indigestion, will go away. Medical people, doctors and nurses particularly, react in quite the opposite way, they get hypochondriacal and think, in the middle of the night, that their pain must be serious and they are likely to die or need an operation.

Cancer, which is to an extent age related, is commoner in older people and usually less malignant than in younger ones. Sadly we don't talk about the cancers that have been cured; we only refer to friends and relatives who have died, often at an age when death from some cause is likely anyway. This gives cancer its feared and sinister reputation, it would be better to refer more to the successful treatments, as do the Americans, because overall about half of all cancers are either treated or controlled successfully and the cure rate would go up with earlier diagnosis and wider discussion.

The successful treatment of many cancers thus depends principally on early diagnosis: which can only begin with the patient's willingness to go to the surgery. I get very cross when, finally cornered, a patient will say 'I didn't like to bother the doctor, he was so busy'. Doctors exist to be reasonably bothered and you employ them through your taxes, to look after you. Medicine is free and is a consumer service and doctors particularly under their new agreements, are, and need to be, consumer orientated.

The cervical or Pap smear is now part of most women's lives, by accepting it they are in fact admitting that they might have early cervical cancer and are prepared to take avoiding action. Breast screening is now available in the NHS, breast cancer affects one in thirteen women and non-cancerous lumps are several times more common. Breast cancer is four times as prevalent as cervical cancer and thus screening could be more valuable if properly used. All breast lumps should be regarded as sinister until proved innocent by investigation. A special X-ray mammograph may reveal early growths too small to be felt.

The great thing about early diagnosis—getting the cancer while it is still small and local—is because successful treatment is much simpler and less radical. Thus a small breast lump can be locally removed without serious distortion of the breast. But achieving this rests with the patient.

I have used breast cancer as an example because it is common but there are diseases other than cancer that also benefit from early diagnosis. Thus it is sensible to be prepared to take all new symptoms that don't have an obvious cause like a recent injury, or don't get better in a few days, to the doctor for evaluation. Common symptoms which need to be looked at early are:

- loss of weight and appetite
- gain in weight without dietary over-indulgence

- persistent headache
- change in sleep pattern, waking early and feeling gloomy
- depression is common, treatable and often missed
- tranquillisers and sleeping pills do not help
- breathlessness, persistent cough and swollen ankles at the end of the day

A mild degree of ankle swelling which has gone by the morning is almost normal in older people. Any bleeding from anywhere, from coughing, vomiting, rectum or vagina, must be reported at once. Any bleeding or pain from a skin lesion or change in size or appearance in the established mole or skin blemish, report at once. Change of bowel habit or difficulty. This can be looseness or constipation or alternate. Most bowel cancers present like this, with pain, discharge or discomfort. If caught early they respond well to surgery. Any pain anywhere which is new and persists for more than a few days, particularly if it is not related to an injury. New lumps or bumps that you can see or feel even if they are painless. 'Old friends' are safe to leave provided they don't change. Pain in the leg or chest on walking or exercise.

The list could be endless but these are the main signals. What it adds up to is to be sensible about any new symptoms. Don't hope that they will go away but get a check on them. Most will turn out to be harmless but it is very much a case of a stitch in time. The onus for threading the needle rests on you.

If you've now been persuaded to face cancer hopefully and not postpone diagnosis, could I be allowed to repeat my suggestion? It can be helpful for a family to define attitudes to serious illness and have a family plan about how you want to be handled. If you are over 80 and develop, say, cancer or a serious stroke, you are quite entitled to decline heroic treatment and ask to fade away peacefully. It would be much easier to be accepted by doctors and others if your wishes are previously recorded. And, of course, you are equally entitled to say 'Don't tell me I don't want to know'.

At long last the doctor/patient relationship is changing for the better, doctors are more willing to discuss symptoms and they are getting more holistic, even to accepting some alternative therapies. In nearly all medical situations there are options as to therapies and surgery. Patients should now expect to participate in the decision taking, having the odds spelt out and the options described and to decide for themselves what option should be taken.

Doctors and patients choose each other and if the relationship is to flourish they must be compatible. It is now much easier to change doctors without their being unreasonable and the more determined of us can help to change their attitude and behaviour by insisting on full discussion of drugs and treatment.

Lastly, it's worth mentioning, firstly that simple screening is now more available and the over 75's should be regularly screened by their GP. I think that it is sensible to know also whether or not blood pressure is normal, that there are no abnormalities like sugar in the urine or changes in the blood chemistry. If you know your vulnerability you can decide on the options more rationally.

15.8   Arthritis and rheumatism

If you go to your doctor with a muscular pain or spasm and if after a thorough probing examination he says 'it's only a touch of rheumatism, take these pills or liniment or use a heat lamp', you know that it's only your rheumatism and that it will hopefully get better fairly soon.

In fact, rheumatism as a disease does not exist. The musculo-skeletal system is a complicated mixture of bones, joints, ligaments, muscles and tendons and often it is very difficult to nail the precise cause of pain. Without this the right specific treatment is hard to prescribe. Rheumatism is an acceptable terminological dumping ground for musculo-skeletal pain of unknown cause which usually gets better at least for the time being. Doctors and patients seem to be happy with it.

All this is particularly true of back pain, lumbago, sciatica, prolapsed disc and so on. Treatments are as many and various as the causes and none of them works all the time. If a precise diagnosis, like a prolapsed disc or obvious arthritis, can be made, at least one knows the problem and the options, although satisfactory treatment may still be difficult.

Also of course in the light of what has been said about tension and anxiety, a lot of muscle pain is due to tension and merits a holistic approach, a pain in the neck is a symbolic condition, reflecting real dis-ease and tension.

15.8.1   Rheumatoid arthritis (RA)

Strictly speaking arthritis means inflammation inside a joint. Rheumatoid arthritis is a common and distressing disease of at present unknown cause. It may have an immunological or allergic basis or it may be infectious. It starts as an inflammation of the tissues around the joints which become very tender and painful and the joint later distorts by scarring. The inflammatory process later involves and indeed may destroy the joints and cause great disability. RA as it is conveniently known, causes much long term suffering and is the main interest of the rheumatologist. On the whole it can be palliated but not cured by drugs and any joint in the body can be involved.

15.8.2   Osteoarthritis (OA)

Osteoarthritis is true arthritis in that it is a wear and tear condition of large joints in which the cartilage which covers the bone ends and allows them to articulate smoothly against each other, gets damaged so that the raw bone ends are then in contact and cause pain.

Old injury, other deformities, like a short leg or twisted spine and plain wear and tear from weight-bearing, pre-dispose to OA. It is thus a disease of older people and mainly involves hips, knees, ankles and of course the spine. It causes creaking and painful joints which often have to be, as it were, wound up in the mornings. It is a common cause of back pain and stiffness which is much more difficult to treat than, say the hip which can now be replaced by an artificial joint. In fact spare part surgery is at its most useful for joint replacement. Hip replacement is now standard worldwide, although there is still room for improvement over the materials used.

The knee replacement is rapidly improving. The knee, because it locks for strength on standing, is a more difficult joint to mimic but technology is improving all the time, and it is an easy joint to get at surgically because it is literally skin deep.

Because they are not weight-bearing shoulder, elbow and wrist joints get less arthritic except after injury, but replacements are now becoming practical for them. In surgical terms a fixed rigid joint may often be less of a hardship than a painful stiff one, so if only one joint like the ankle is involved there may be case for fusing it. In the old days this was a possibility for reducing the pain of an arthritic hip.

Active treatment apart, there are two points for living with osteo-arthritis. One is to keep one's weight well down to reduce the load on the damaged joint. In fact many arthritic hips may be caused by years of overload this way. The second, and this goes particularly for backs and knees, is to maintain muscle strength by special exercises. Pain is biologically protective, it calls for help and in various ways like spasm, stops the painful parts being moved. This means that the muscles weaken from disuse, making the joints then more vulnerable.

Thus, for the painful or injured knee, perhaps a torn cartilage, the big thigh muscles (called the quadriceps because there are four of them) attached to the knee, weaken very rapidly and waste away. Similarly, with a painful back the long spinal muscles weaken and cease to be protective, possibly causing further injury.

Any significant arthritis should be X-rayed and investigated by a specialist and regularly reviewed as to possible new treatment.

15.9   Coronary thrombosis

About a quarter of men get a coronary before retiring age. The coronary arteries supply the heart muscle, they are so called because they run round the heart like a crown. Thrombosis is the name given to an artery blocked by a blood clot, usually due to disease of the artery wall, called arteriosclerosis.

Coronary thrombosis, then, is a blockage of the coronary arteries which damages or destroys the heart muscle supplied. It is a manifestation of arteriosclerosis which is a generalised disease but in younger people it may be confined to the coronary arteries.

Known as Coronary Heart Disease (CHD) it is caused by a number of risk factors, like smoking, high animal fat content in the diet, lack of exercise, genetic inheritance and so on. Vulnerability is clearly lifestyle related and to a considerable extent, the disease should be preventable.

Men surviving to retirement are clearly not particularly coronary prone, but should not take risks like smoking, obesity or lack of exercise.

15.10   Strokes

A stroke is the name given to damage to the brain from failure of blood supply. This can be either from thrombosis, as in coronaries, or from rupture or haemorrhage, which damages the brain. A stroke is usually a manifestation of arteriosclerosis and hypertension. It is commonest after retirement age. The early detection and treatment of hypertension significantly reduces the incidence of stroke, an argument in favour of regular screening or health checks.

The effects of a stroke depend entirely on the position and extent of the arterial and brain injury. If the speech centre is involved there will be speech defect. If parts of the cortex are involved on one or other side, there will be paralysis. Any part of the brain can be damaged so that strokes come, suddenly and unexpectedly, with a wide range of symptoms; muscle paralysis and speech defects being the commonest. Massive strokes are obviously more or less instantly fatal although deep coma can lead to death from pneumonia. Often they are confined to one side of the brain, paralysing the opposite side of the body. This is called hemiplegia.

Because of its structure the brain cannot repair or replace itself, recovery of function thus depends on re-educating residual brain and muscle power, to make the best of what is left. It is a long and demanding process, depending on the determination of the patient and the willingness of friends and relatives to help and encourage the return of speech and movement.

Mini strokes, however, often leave little disability and blood vessel spasm can mimic a stroke with often complete recovery. The Heart, Chest and Stroke Society can be very helpful with advice.

15.11   Parkinson's Disease (PD)

Now that more people are living longer, Parkinson's Disease seems to be more common. Certainly after a great deal of research much more is now known about its causation and hence treatment, although now that the latter has become more complicated, with a wider range of drugs, much remains to be learnt.

Deep inside the brain is an area called the substantia nigra which deals with dopamine and related substances. This area influences muscle control and the disease which has a range of symptoms is character-ised by muscle rigidity, tremor and a characteristic posture and fixed expressionless face. There is also a peculiar way of walking in which the patient leans forward and looks as if he's chasing his centre of gravity. It is because of these systems that it is known as paralysis agitans.

It is gradually, over years, progressive, but can, by skilful manipula-tion of drugs, be controlled for a very long time. It is more common in men than women and being slowly progressive may lead ultimately to high dependency. The Parkinson's Disease Society can be helpful.

15.12   Special problems—women

Because of their complicated hormone cycles, women can suffer hormone upsets before and after the menopause. These can, if not treated, make life very difficult for them. Thus in middle and indeed younger life, Pre-Menstrual Tension (PMT) causes serious and disabling mood change. A lot is now known about the causation and control of the condition and many centres have special PMT clinics.

Later, with the loss of fertility and the cessation of menstruation, comes the menopause. There again hormone changes produce physical and emotional symptoms which can be controlled by treatment known as hormone replacement therapy (HRT). This can be quite important because the basic changes also relate to cholesterol levels in the blood and hence coronary risk and bone calcium concentration. HRT appears to influence both these beneficially and may thus be indicated without other symptoms. The problem is that HRT involves the continuation of menstruation and as with contraceptive pill may have effects on blood clotting and possibly cancer risk. The best use of HRT is still under investigation but as was said earlier, osteoporosis (brittle bones) is important enough to merit prevention.

It is perhaps hard on women that most doctors are men, not particularly sympathetic to their seemingly emotional problems. Special clinics exist and the BUPA Medical Centre and others have admirable leaflets on PMT, HRT and breast cancer.

Breast cancer and cervical smears have already been discussed which leads, as a special problem, to the uterus or womb. This is a complicated organ very much under hormone control and undergoing cyclic change throughout reproductive life. Because of this and for other reasons, like benign fibroid tumours and the two cancers of the neck and the body of the womb, the uterus can cause a lot of problems.

If these occur while reproduction is still possible, ie early to mid reproductive life, the problems or the treatment may limit fertility and the treatment compromise be difficult to decide on. After this, however, removal of the uterus (hysterectomy) is a relatively simple operation with a few physical side effects.

The trouble is, however, that, rather like mastectomy (removal of the breast) the uterus, not surprisingly, is of great emotional significance as a symbol of femininity and reproductive capacity. This means that sympathetic counselling before and after hysterectomy is desirable but not very often available.

In fact, properly done, a hysterectomy doesn't interfere with sexual activity; obviously it stops menstruation and removes the risk of relatively common cancers. If HRT controls osteoporosis there could be a case for palliative hysterectomy to deal with the menstrual problems.

A new technique which can be done on a day basis, using a laser beam to destroy the lining of the uterus, looks as if it may partially replace hysterectomy and the related emotional reactions.

15.13 Special problems—men

Men, having a less complicated reproductive apparatus which only contributes semen without having to nurture a foetus, have many fewer specific problems. The male menopause does not exist (various mid-life crises may, but they are not hormone or menstrual related) but there is a prostate which can cause problems.

The prostate is a small gland situated below the bladder surrounding the exit tube, the urethra. Apart from contributing to seminal fluid, the prostate has no great function. Unfortunately, however, it commonly enlarges in later life. The reason for this enlargement is not known and has little effect except on the urethra which gets partially blocked by the pressure from the enlarged gland. This causes urinary symptoms which have to be dealt with to prevent infection and protect the kidneys from back pressure.

Treatment involves removing all or part of the prostate to 'unblock the drain'. This used to be a difficult operation producing consider-able discomfort but now it can be done through the penis and without opening the bladder. Using either a diathermy hotwire or now a laser beam, the obstruction can be removed and even if it should recur, the operation can be repeated. Thus treating an enlarged prostate is now a relatively simple procedure in experienced hands.

Cancer of the prostate is relatively common and difficult to treat because removing the whole prostate without destroying the sphincters which control bladder emptying is not easy. At this moment in time there is considerable controversy about the best treatment at the various stages of what is usually a slow growing cancer in an older man, ie he may easily die of something else, so wait and see what happens. One can then deal with, on their merits, the spread and complications should they occur. This would seem to be a matter for expert advice and probably a second opinion because the best methods for later prostatic cancer treatment are not yet very clear.

Mythology used to have it that a prostate operation destroyed sexual activity in a man. It doesn't. It may produce sterility at an age when reproduction should probably be discouraged anyway. The ejaculatory ducts which pass through the prostate may be destroyed by the operation, ejaculation then takes place into the bladder.

Vasectomy is now a popular method of contraception when a couple have had the number of children they want. The trouble is that there is a high divorce rate, then maybe a second marriage that wants to have a child. So perhaps there is a case for not having a vasectomy too soon. There seem to be no ill effects and techniques for reversing the operation are now being developed and are quite often successful.

Further reading

Are You Managing Your Health? by Beric Wright (Industrial Society and Allied Dunbar)

16   Mental health and outlook

Of all the parts of the body the brain is the most mature at birth and subsequently grows the least. At birth most of its main cellular components are in place and the circuits are there ready to open up in response to learning and experience. Restrictions of sensory experience in early life can, it is said, have a limiting effect on the number of circuits which finally develop. Hence the need for stimulation in early life.

It is also believed that a few brain cells begin to drop off early and this loss of neurones goes on all the time until death. Provided there is no overt disease like alcoholism, Alzheimers or what is now called multiple infarct—previously senile—dementia, people can remain mentally competent and alert for over a century.

But there are changes in the brain which it is useful to understand and live with. Simplistically the brain is a cross between a computer and switchboard and like all electronic devices it becomes less reliable as it ages. Connections don't go through so accurately and lines get crossed. This change has two main effects on performance particularly as regards short-term memory (STM) and reflex or automatic response.

16.1   Short-term memory (STM)

Memory can conveniently be arbitrarily divided into short (in the here and now) and long term (for past events) memory. My ancient mother could give graphic accounts of her early life but couldn't remember if I have been in to see her that morning.

We don't know exactly how memory works at a cellular level but it must be a precisely indexed, rapidly retrievable library of knowledge and experience.

I'm sure that all readers moderately past middle-age have experienced being interrupted in the middle of doing something, eg by having to answer the door bell, and completely forgetting what they were at. Their short-term memories have failed for this event.

Two things probably contribute to this failure, the first is that because of the slowing down and aging the connections don't get through, as also happens when you can't remember something on the tip of your tongue. The other is more speculative, but I think it is due to the fact that the memory bank is full and it's more difficult to find 'filing space' for that particular new piece of activity. This may be the reason why youngsters respond so quickly to new ideas, they have less experience to work through.

The answer is to take more trouble to remember, or not to forget; this is called imprinting. What you have to do is to proceed on the basis that you might well forget and write it down or repeat it over to yourself and then it will stick. This is quite important because the art of growing old gracefully is to appear less stupid than you are.

I find two things about my STM, the first is that it is subject to fatigue, worse when I'm tired and at the end of the day or the week, the other is that it is irritatingly unpredictable, so much so that as I get older I have to try and remember to do only one thing, or think of one thing at a time; otherwise the first thing may be pushed out and forgotten by the second.

I mention this for two reasons, first for reassurance that it has nothing to do with dementia—you can be dotty without being demented—and secondly in terms of every day efficiency, it is helpful to understand and minimise the effects. Dementia is briefly mentioned later.

16.2   Reflex response

We act and respond to pressures and challenges through a series of automatic reflex actions originally described by the Russian Pavlov. As the brain ages, these, as with memory, slow down and become less reliable. Two examples (and there are plenty of others), will illustrate what happens.

Many of us have been stuck when driving behind an elderly driver who seems unable to get into the main road. Such drivers appear to be dithering. In fact what is happening is that the scenario on the main road is changing more quickly than their response rate can adjust to. Their reflexes are slowing down. Also because it becomes less comfortable, they may not be driving enough to retain their skills. All skills do require practice or training to keep up to scratch. Similarly and more often, it will inevitably take an older person longer deciding and then trying to cross a complicated road. As pedestrians and drivers you need to be aware of this. Everything does take a bit longer as we age, and there is not much you can do about it.

16.3 Mental activity

A lot of research has demonstrated that older people can learn new skills and acquire new knowledge, but they also benefit from different teaching methods. School day 'chalk and talk' is not necessarily the best way for adults. Numerous adult education courses, the Open University and more recently the University of the Third Age (U3A) have demonstrated both the success and the possibilities of learning in later life.

Like other body systems the brain has to be kept on its toes by being given new things to think about and puzzle over. Mental inertia can be as debilitating as physical inactivity. Some people keep lively and active into later life because it is their nature to remain involved, others of us would benefit from trying harder as a regular discipline.

To remain dynamic all living things need to be constantly challenged by their environment. For those of us in developed countries, this challenge comes from our psycho-social and interpersonal, rather than our physical, environment. Life without new challenge—the same old routine day after day—is inevitably boring. Coping successfully with retirement or indeed with mid-life ennui relates strongly, I am sure, to looking for new challenges to stimulate mental and physical life. Do something exciting, get out of the rut into the sunshine of new endeavour. Even before retirement changing jobs can work wonders for well being. So, too, can getting out of a boring or unsatisfactory relationship.

Taking trouble to keep in touch with younger people, including young children, is protection against fogeyism. I'm sure that the key to successful survival lies in continued and new mental and physical activity. Sticking in the mud promotes inertia and sticks in the mud are both bored and boring.

16.4   Dementia

Although dementia in older people has been a well described medical condition for very many years it has recently become more important and prominent for two reasons. First because the condition seems to have become more common and secondly, because a seemingly new and very similar disease—Alzheimer's Disease (AD)—has been separated and defined more accurately. The effect of this newer definition is that what used to be called senile dementia has now being separated into two different conditions—Alzheimer's Disease (AD) and Multiple Infarct Dementia (MID).

Both are age related although AD tends to start younger and progress more rapidly, MID may in fact remain stable for longer periods. Some, but not all, AD runs in families.

The reason for their increasing incidence and importance is, sadly, due to better living conditions and increased life expectancy. More people, particularly women, are living long enough to become demented. It now looks as if about 20% of those living to beyond 80 or 85, will become demented. This of course poses very considerable personal and community problems which are only just beginning to be faced. Also the mere possibility of being afflicted creates anxiety.

But because of the increase in longevity and incidence, many of us now in early retirement have been faced directly or indirectly with the very real problems of coping with a demented elderly relative. To give but one simple example, my wife's mother was here for four days over Christmas and was fetched and carried by her son. She is classically and very irritatingly demented and later on in the evening she had gone home, she rang up to say she was miserable and had been alone all over Christmas.

MID is a manifestation of arteriosclerosis and often related to raised blood pressure. Cognitive functions of the cerebral cortex are disturbed by what seems to be a random distribution of mini strokes (infarct being the name given to the effect of a blocked blood vessel as with coronary thrombosis). As has been said, MID comes on later in life and is less progressive. An aunt of mine has just died after 20 years in a nursing home, not knowing where she was or recognising visitors. The main effect of both AD and MID is the loss of short-term memory. The sufferers can only remember what is in their minds at that moment. This is why they repeat questions and follow one about. They do this because it is, at that moment, their only contact with reality: without it they are 'floating in space and very frightened'.

AD appears to be a specific condition with characteristic changes in cortical brain cells, which can be recognised under the microscope. It may be related to the metabolism of aluminium and it might become treatable. In its early stages the symptoms are very similar to MID. As it is more progressive, total confusion and other disabilities lead to total dependency.

As far as the patient is concerned it doesn't at the moment make much difference which disease one has and treatment can only be palliative. Experts argue about critical points of diagnostic separation and hopefully the current research effort will bring classification and better management.

As I said earlier, there is no correlation between normal STM loss and full-blown dementia. But this brief account has been added now, because of the increasing incidence and general anxiety about the possibility of becoming demented.

Because it will become commoner as we all go on living longer, the possibility is a good reason for making an enduring power of attorney. The Alzheimer's Disease Society has an excellent advisory service and admirable literature and they also help over advising on long stay accommodation. The Abbeyfield Society has a very helpful leaflet on confusion in the elderly, on which this account is based.

16.5 Stress

Stress is an overworked phrase, which, as it is rarely properly defined, is so often variably interpreted to cover a spectrum of cause and effect; from someone who is successfully holding down a demanding job to another who gives in to the mildest challenge. It has also become a cult phrase, it being fashionable to be stressed, and one sometimes gets the impression that ambitious executives would feel unsuccessful if they were not stressed.

Very briefly, because this is not the place for a detailed account of stress, all living things are in conflict with their environment, competing with each other and against other species in the necessities of life. In Darwinian terms, evolution is powered by the survival of the fittest, the weak going to the wall, taking their genes with them.

The upshot of this, particularly for man, is that life demands challenge to keep it tuned up and lively. Thus challenge is a biological necessity but obviously if it is important there will also be an equally biological defence mechanism to protect against 'over stretch'. This defence we now call a stress reaction.

The importance of the distinction between challenge and stress is that the latter is a manifestation of inability to cope with that particular situation. Successful people may be tired but their morale is high. Stress is thus a biological admission of defeat, but life is not quite that simple because higher organisms, mammals and certainly man, react as a whole and the reaction is subconscious. You don't necessarily know why you get a headache when you don't want to go out, or a child gets tummy pain when it's frightened of school. This is, however, what happens and another complication, that some doctors still find difficult, is that some of the reactions may be traditionally physical, like asthma or duodenal ulcer, while others may be behavioural, like anxiety, depression, insomnia or just indigestion and irritability.

Another factor complicates the issue and this is the personality and past experiences of the individual, ie extroverts react differently from introverts and highly strung, anxious folk find life more difficult than the calm and placid, who take it all as it comes. Thus stress thresholds differ widely from person to person and time to time.

The other corollary of this concept of stress is that the whole of life is involved, not necessarily one segment of it. Domestic conflict or anxiety feeds into the office and vice versa. Similarly, we all have different skills and thresholds, are good at some things and poor at others. But stress is basically an inability to cope with some part of one's life. Experts may be good at their craft but hopeless at relationships. All of this is the basis of Holism, one needs to know the 'why' of symptoms before writing a prescription. And very often revealing cause and effect will make a prescription unnecessary. Traditionally patients are expected to present pain in some or another form to the doctor, who in turn provides a healing medicine. Now we are beginning to offer (and patients are demanding) talk, rather than drugs.

I believe that disease is dis-ease and that one has to look at the lifestyle and personality related causes of symptoms. In many ways there is more to be learned from those who don't get ill, than from those who are diseased. There must be an in-built resistance or immunity which is a mixture of genes, personality and experience. Wellness is a balacing act between challenge and resistance: disease can be physical or behavioural and often an amalgam of both. Clearly, as has been said, basic personality traits are a major determinant of thresholds.

Stress and wellness are discussed at greater length in the author's recently published *Are You Managing Your Health?* (Industrial Society and Allied Dunbar).

Relating stress to retirement in broad outline is relatively easy. If work has been increasingly demanding, frustrating, boring and hence stressful, retirement will come as a relief, anxiety will melt away and life will become fun.

Another point to understand is that the challenge may well cause fatigue even if it is successfully coped with. Fatigue is not the same as stress but it does lower resistance and the stress threshold.

When I had been retired for about six months and had recovered from the shock of no longer being work programmed, I suddenly realised, on the train one day, that I felt different and better. Analysing this suggested that I was no longer tired. Busy people at the end of their working lives get used to being chronically fatigued, it does take time to recover completely.

Going back to retirement stress, if one fears, resents and has given no thought to retirement, when it comes, there will be fear and resentment. Partners will wonder what on earth you will do: this will of course be more stressful than work was. Hence the value of pre-retirement counselling courses and books like this, in alerting readers to the problems and possibilities of their third age.

When you no longer have work to go to, you suddenly realise how it has motivated and programmed your life. Now, perhaps for the first time, you have to be entirely self programming, you have to pull your finger out and put things in the diary. Maybe your partner will take over the role of the secretary. But most people who have worked hard and enjoyed it, find this sudden drop to total self motivation stressful. As in the work situation, underemployment is just as frustrating and stressful as over employment.

16.6   Anxiety

Anxiety can be largely considered as a manifestation of stress, in that one worries on the whole about things or situations that appear or feel in some way threatening. Also, of course, anxiety is very much a reflection of personality, strong people tend not to worry much, weak, fussy people tie themselves into continuous knots worrying over things that seem trivial to the rest of us.

The main feature of anxiety, however, is that it causes tension: being screwed up does exactly what it implies and tension is painful—headache, migraine, tummy colic, muscle spasms, etc, are all common in stress related tension pains. Acute anxiety or panic states for justifiable or seemingly trivial reasons, can thus be totally disorganising.

But at ordinary levels of personality and relationships, anxiety is a common cause of stress, much of which is hidden because of our reluctance to discuss problems and grievances. Tensions get bottled up and produce dis-ease.

The point has already been made that well-being in retirement, particularly as age advances, benefits from minimising stress and anxiety. For instance, wives who have themselves plenty to do worry about the effects of retirement on their husband. In our society we may marry for better or worse, but not for seven lunches a week. Seeing too much of each other can be stressful.

Similarly, and this point has been mentioned in relation to financial planning and Wills, women worry particularly about becoming widows. I mention this again to emphasise the point that difficult though it might be, and some families are better at this than others, it is helpful to make relationships as open as possible.

Discuss grievances before they become problems. We all irritate each other in relatively trivial ways, and if this is the case say so, rather than let it smoulder. And if there is a real problem counsellors who are trained to define situations rather than present solutions, can be very sympathetically helpful. RELATE which used to be the Marriage Guidance Council, has a vast experience of helping people in this way to discuss their problems.

16.7   Relaxation and coping

Stress has always been part of life and living and we do like to think we are more stressed than our forebears, which is probably untrue, although today's stresses may be more complex. There is no doubt that there is a lot of anxiety and tension about, from work and home. Obviously some people are more highly strung than others. These people can often be considerably helped by being taught to relax and to include overt relaxation in their daily life patterns by, say, meditating. We tend to think of ourselves as stressed but it is honest to also analyse whether we are stressors. What am I like to be married to or work for, is a useful question to ask yourself from time to time.

There are a number of techniques available from transcendental meditation (TM) to bio-feedback and various forms of yoga. An organisation, Relaxation for Living, specialises in assessing and teaching various techniques of relaxation, including doing without tranquillisers. If you have a tension problem which persists into retirement it is well worth seeking their help. Similarly if specific situations produce tension you can get help in learning what are called coping skills to recognise and deal with them as you can for phobias.

Thinking broadly about these problem areas is useful at the start of retirement, because work does to a degree protect from having to face difficulties in interpersonal relations. Work associates are no longer there and you need all the friends and contacts you have, they need to be cherished and worked at. It is not easy for instance, to have adult relationships with children now grown up, and their basic relationships with you may reflect on the way grandchildren are approached and recognised. Most of us are enthusiastic grandparents and look forward to having more time: a few others are not so keen and prefer to get on with their own lives. I have learnt from others that it may be wise to let it be known what your attitude to being a grandparent is when you retire, because it may be assumed that you are now more available than you want to be, so make a benchmark.

Postscript

This book makes no apology for having mentioned planning dozens of times. The key for enjoying a fulfilled and happy retirement will largely be due to the way in which you approach that period of your life.

The 1991 census will, in stark contrast to the first census in 1801, produce a mass of statistics which will take nearly two years to fully process and publish. However, there seems no doubt that the results will confirm the trend of an aging Britain with more people retired, yet more people in work.

A growing trend will be for that (currently) small group of people who have retired from their main, and probably stressful, career, now to have started their own businesses or be providing consultancy services in the field of their expertise or simply working in a less demanding position with a firm primarily for the social contact and business interest.

When the census bicentenary comes round in the year 2001 what will you be doing? Still at work frantically balancing business or home interests, sitting by the fire wondering what you will be doing next week and the week after that, or perhaps planning your campaign to become a district councillor or school governor at the next elections?

To a very large extent, the choice is yours.

Glossary of financial terms

AVC

Additional voluntary contributions to an employer's pension scheme. These contributions are paid from your income into your company pension scheme. Separate Free Standing AVC schemes are available from insurance companies and other financial institutions.

Accumulation and maintenance trusts

A special type of trust which is favourably treated for IHT purposes.

Age relief

A tax allowance available to those aged 65 or more provided that their income does not exceed certain limits.

Annuities

A policy sold by an insurance company under which you (and possibly your spouse) receive a stated sum for the rest of your life or a specified period.

Appropriate personal pensions

A special type of personal pension to be used for contracting out of SERPS.

Basic retirement pension

The State pension payable to everyone attaining state retirement age. Usually called the Old Age Pension.

Buy-out bonds

An arrangement under which an individual can transfer his entitlement under a former employer's pension scheme to an individual policy.

Commuting pension

A pension is commuted when the individual takes a tax free lump sum in lieu of all or part of his entitlement.

Contracting out

The option available to all members of SERPS to opt out in favour of a personal pension.

Deed of family arrangement

An agreement reached by beneficiaries of a person's estate under which the provisions of the Will are varied for tax and personal financial planning reasons.

Discretionary trust

This is a type of trust where the trustees do not have to pay income to a particular beneficiary but can choose each year how they allocate income to members of a class of potential beneficiaries.

Domicile

Domicile is not necessarily connected with where you currently live, and should not be confused with tax residence. Domicile is, broadly, the territory which can be regarded as your natural home and in which (apart from occasional absences) you intend to remain indefinitely. Your domicile of origin is determined at birth and, in most circumstances, it will be the domicile of your father. Domicile is not solely determined by nationality or by place of birth, though these will in many cases be the same as your domicile. Most UK expatriates are, therefore, of UK domicile.

Double taxation agreements

These provide relief to an individual who has income which arises in a foreign country especially where the income is being taxed in that country. Relief can be given either by offsetting the foreign tax paid when calculating taxable income, or by averaging the overall tax payable at the rate applicable here. Similar arrangements may cover people who retire overseas and have income arising in the UK (note that not all countries have a treaty with the UK).

Equalisation

Dividing assets of an estate equally between husband and wife to utilise both nil rate bands.

Equities

This is a general name given to ordinary shares issued by quoted companies. Their value rises and falls according to the company's trading results, the Stock Market in general etc. The term equity is meant to distinguish such investments from loan stocks and other fixed interest investments.

Estate

This is a technical term for the property which you own at the date of death and trust property where you are entitled to any income.

Executors

People who administer a Will.

Exempt gilts

These are gilts where the interest is exempt from UK tax if the owner is not resident or ordinarily resident in the UK.

Frozen pension

Pension benefits arising from a former employment which will become payable when the individual reaches retirement age.

Gilts

Also known as UK government stocks. These are loan stocks issued by HM Government. They usually carry a fixed rate of interest and are redeemable at a particular date. Some gilts are, however, linked to inflation, ie 'index-linked' gilts.

Golden handshake

A lump sum paid voluntarily on an employment ceasing. Also known as termination payments.

Grant of representation

Documentation enabling estate to be realised and distributed.

Gross fund

One that is not subject to tax, for example a pension fund.

Inheritance tax (IHT)

Death duty, replaced capital transfer tax (which replaced estate duty) in March 1986.

Insurance bonds

An investment which takes the form of a non-qualifying insurance policy.

Intestacy

This applies where a person dies without making a valid Will.

Invalidity benefit

State benefit for people suffering long term incapacity. It is non taxable.

Managed funds

A term commonly used to describe a type of unit linked fund offered by insurance companies, where the insurance company seeks to achieve a balanced portfolio with some of the fund being invested in property, equities, foreign companies, gilts and cash deposits.

Maximum investment plan

A qualifying ten year endowment insurance policy.

National Savings Certificates

These are investments offered by the Government which provide a tax free return over periods of up to five years.

Net relevant earnings

Earnings from a non-pensionable employment or business less certain deductions such as expenses, trading losses, capital allowances etc.

Nil rate band

This is the amount of an estate that can pass on death before attracting IHT.

Offshore 'roll-up' funds

Mutual funds (similar in concept to unit trusts) based in a tax haven such as the Isle of Man or the Channel Islands. Income earned on the fund's portfolio is not paid out as dividends but is accumulated or 'rolled-up'.

Open market options

These are options under certain types of individual or personal pension plans whereby the individual can 'shop around' at the time of retirement and transfer the value of the policy to the company which offers the best annuity rates.

Personal Equity Plan (PEP)

Tax exempt savings plan linked to shares and unit trusts.

Personal pension plan

Individual pension scheme designed for those who are self-employed or in a non pensionable employment.

Private health insurance (PHI)

Individual insurance policy to provide income in the event of long term illness or disability.

Residence

A concept used to determine under which country's taxation laws you are liable. Although there are complex and differing rules, residence is generally determined by where you actually live in any tax year. In circumstances where this is not clear, you are likely to be declared resident for tax purposes in any country in which you spend more than six months in any tax year (although the legislation differs from country to country, 183 days is the period often adopted for determining residence).

Reservation of benefit

If property is given away but some form of benefit is reserved by the donor, then the gift is null and void for IHT purposes.

Retirement relief

Substantial capital gains tax allowances for those disposing of a business on retirement.

Salary sacrifice

An arrangement whereby an individual gives up some of his salary, with the amount that has been given up being paid into a pension scheme.

SERPS

State Earnings Related Pension Scheme.

Tax Exempt Special Savings Account (TESSA)

Tax exempt savings plan linked to building society or money market interest bearing funds.

Transfer values

A payment made from a former employer's pension scheme to secure benefits under your present employer's pension scheme. Also transfers can be made between self-employed pension policies to secure the best annuity rate at retirement.

Trust

A trust, or settlement, is an arrangement under which property passes to trustees for the benefit of beneficiaries.

Trustee

The custodian of trust assets and property.

Unit trusts

A type of investment where investors join together to invest via a pooled 'fund'.

Checklist of essential information

Where my Documents may be found

Name:

Date:

My deed/safe box may be found:

The key may be found:

Key number:

....

My Birth/Marriage certificates may be found:

My passport may be found:

My life assurance and disability policies may be found:

My car insurance policy may be found:

My home contents insurance policy may be found:

My house building insurance may be found:

My shares/investments certificates may be found:

Accountant:

Name:

Address:

Phone No:

Solicitor:

Name:

Address:

Phone No:

Other Adviser: (eg Stockbroker)

Name:

Address:

Phone No:

In the event of my death please contact:

Name:

Address:

Phone No:

Name:

Address:

Phone No:

Employer's Details:

Company/Works Name:

Payroll/Works No:

National Insurance No:

Phone Number:

Please contact:

I am/am not a member of a company pension scheme.

Life assurance policies and pension plans:

Company	Policy Number	On whose life
....
....
....
....
....

Disability Cover (PHI):

Policy No:

Company:

Home:

Mortgage with (Building Society, Bank etc)

Address:

Phone No:

Mortgage ref. No:

The Deeds are with:

Building Insurance with (Company Name):

Address:

Policy No:

Sum assured	Reason for purchase	Who to contact
....		
....		
....		
....		
....		

Contents Insurance with:

Address:

Policy No:

Investment Property:

I own the following property (other than my main residence):

I am the sole/joint owner with:

of:

The deeds are located:

The mortgage is with:

Address:

Phone No:

Investments:

I have the following investments (eg shares, unit-trusts, premium bonds, national savings certificates, etc.):

Investment   Certificate Number

....

....

....

....

....

....

....

Income Tax:

The tax office which deals with my affairs is:

Phone No:

Reference No:

My Will:

The original of my Will is with/placed in:

The Will is dated:

The Will was drawn up by:

Address:

The Executors are:

Bank Account(s):

These are held at:

Bank Name:

Address:

Phone No:

Account No:

Bank Name:

Address:

Phone No:

Account No:

Index